VEXED

VEXED

Ethics Beyond Political Tribes

JAMES MUMFORD

BLOOMSBURY CONTINUUM
LONDON • OXFORD • NEW YORK • NEW DELHI • SYDNEY

BLOOMSBURY CONTINUUM
Bloomsbury Publishing Plc
50 Bedford Square, London, WC1B 3DP, UK

BLOOMSBURY, BLOOMSBURY CONTINUUM and the Diana logo are
trademarks of Bloomsbury Publishing Plc

First published in Great Britain 2020

A catalogue record for this book is available from the British Library

Library of Congress Cataloguing-in-Publication data has been applied for

ISBN: HB: 978-1-4729-6634-6; eBook: 978-1-4729-6635-3;
ePDF: 978-1-4729-6636-0

2 4 6 8 10 9 7 5 3 1

Typeset by Deanta Global Publishing Services, Chennai, India
Printed and bound in Great Britain by CPI Group (UK) Ltd, Croydon CR0 4YY

To find out more about our authors and books visit www.bloomsbury.com
and sign up for our newsletters

For Patricia Park (1933–2018)
A great wit, a great woman

'Sit down a while,
And let us once again assail your ears
That are so fortified against our story'

William Shakespeare, *Hamlet*, Act I, sc. i

CONTENTS

INTRODUCTION

PACKAGE-DEAL ETHICS

I'll put it bluntly. Politically, I don't like my options. Growing up in this giddy world – b. 1981 – I've become increasingly dissatisfied with the alternatives on offer. Because there aren't very many. Deep polarization has delivered unacceptable options.

And not just at a party-political level – the dearth of boxes on the ballot paper. The real source of my frustration is the way every conceivable position on controversial *moral* issues has been bundled up into 'package deals' that I'm supposed to choose between. This clustering of causes across the political spectrum is the legacy the boomers bequeathed to us, and it's got me all riled up.

My political identification is supposed to determine every view I take on the most fundamental questions I face. Say I'm on the Left. Because of the way positions have been packaged, the way I vote means I'm urged to press ACCEPT ALL to the terms and conditions of the whole deal: to sign off on every part of the platform. So, I passionately opposed the invasion of Iraq and defend affirmative action to the hilt. Am I simply to inherit an affirmative view of the legalization of drugs? Or maybe I am conservative. I worry about levels of immigration. I bemoan the rise of identity politics. Why am I then supposed to support greater sanctions on welfare for the unemployed?

It was a while before I was able to trace my dissatisfaction to its source – this packaging of positions. In 2013 I moved to the US. I am British, but I also believe in America. I had lived there before – as a child on the West Coast, in the Midwest for a time as a teenager, on the East Coast as a graduate student – and had always been impressed and inspired by how sanguine were the people I met, how open. I liked their awareness of and investment in the American project itself. This time, though, the climate felt different. It may well have been because previously I had been inexcusably oblivious to the volatility of 'race relations'. But now I was struck by the volatility of 'race relations'. And I was overwhelmed by the extremity of polarization. I knew about this in theory. But now I saw for real what it looked like for people to be socially divided along political lines – the faculty ostracizing the professor on the other side of the aisle; churches so engulfed by their division they ignored their *raison d'être*; family members simply disliking each other; and dinner parties where there were no debates because no one from the opposite end of the political spectrum had been invited.

But what struck me wasn't just the partisanship, and its effects on how relationships fared and institutions functioned. It was the range of issues that had come to be enveloped by ideology. The 'sites of contestation' weren't just about matters of state – about the federal budget or Iran's nuclear programme. Thinking had become radically dichotomized about the most intimate quandaries, the most acute dilemmas, the weightiest of controversies – birth and death, growing up and getting old, race and gender, sexuality, family, our obligations to those near and far, what I do with my body and what I do with my wallet. Morality had become thoroughly politicized. Two opposing political visions governed how to act, and how to think about how to act.

Then, the more I thought about the separating out into packages of so many positions on the most existential and important questions, the more I thought about the combinations. And the stranger they seemed.

One of the things I was constantly riveted by in the US was the bumper sticker, one of the most familiar badges of identity. Those colourful if often weathered symbols, captions, emblems and jokes that drivers affix to their rear bumpers and other parts of their car's anatomy attest to far more than partisan affiliations and the onset of the latest election cycle. Alongside partisan convictions are environmental, social or cultural ones, blazing forth people's highest ideals and principles for all the passing world to see. You wear your heart on the boot of your car.

But what is most revealing about these stickers is the company they keep on each individual car. You pull up at the traffic lights. On your right is a car juxtaposing 'Liberals Take and Spend. Conservatives Protect and Serve' with 'Pro Guns. Pro God. Pro Life'. On your left is a car displaying a rainbow flag alongside 'Buy Fresh Buy Local', 'No Nukes' and 'Co-Exist'. Those stances may be ideologically aligned. But do they imply each other? Why should being religious preclude buying fresh, local produce? Why should a dedication to diversity commit you to unilateral disarmament?

Last year I returned home from the States. I'll pretend it was a protest move against the political climate, rather than because I couldn't land a job and my visa was about to expire. I had mixed feelings about departing. I was having to leave a country I love so much, but I would not miss its political climate. So I disembarked, thinking I had left the culture wars behind, only to find them staring me in the face.

It turned out that while I was away from the UK there had been some kind of referendum on whether to leave the European Union, and the country, by the slimmest of margins, had voted in favour. This book is not about my views on Brexit. But what I had not been prepared for was the character of the political cleavage. Just as in the States, people were socially divided on political grounds. Profound disagreement about politics had morphed into hatred of people. Groups were closing ranks; families had been shaken to the core. When I got home, I found that intense polarization was not only an American phenomenon. We may not have AR-15s on our streets. We may not have pro-life marches in our capital. Polarization may not correlate with political parties in so straightforward a way. But what had been both exposed and exacerbated was a brutal political antagonism.

What we also have, I realized, are package deals. Included within them might be slightly different positions. But the dynamic is the same. If you are a Remainer, you are supposed to hold a range of other views that have been bundled together, while the formation of a Brexiteer identity has served freshly to weld together a number of distinctly conservative positions. Here, too, right and left are ideologies proposing ideas not just on policy but on identity, not just who we vote for but how we live.

———

This book is an attempt to wrest myself free of these package deals. I want to affirm certain fundamental principles on the Left and then question why those principles are expressed in some positions and ignored in others. And vice versa: I want to ask why the most compelling conservative principles are not expressed across the board. The aim, I should say, is not to point out inconsistency for its own sake – consistent worldviews can be wicked! My aim in ensuring I haven't subscribed to a package deal is motivated by the assumption that a view can't be right simply because it has been tacked onto another one for contingent historical reasons.

In their quest for power, politicians build coalitions, make compromises, pander to different interests. That's their business. I get it. What I object to is when they paper over the differences and pretend that this amalgam of views creates a unified whole. What I object to is ideological amnesia, their deliberate attempt to make us forget that our intellectual settlement is a direct result of Cut-and-Paste.

DYING TO BELONG

The reason I personally find it difficult to wrest myself free of the package deals is because I want mates. I want to be liked. I want to belong. I want a place in the world, a way to appear in public. A context. All too often I have found the price of individualism too high, contrarianism too costly. Consequently, I have to confess, I have ended up pandering to all parties, trying to be all things to all people.

So, with my friends on the Left I pose as a Remainer appalled by the xenophobes who won the referendum and are now doing their level best to ruin the country – closing Britain for business and forging a freshly antagonistic posture towards the world that will most certainly prove disastrous as we move forward to navigate the perilous waters of the twenty-first century. When I'm in the States, I saunter the lawns of elite colleges and peer down from ivory towers, emitting grave murmurs of agreement to my liberal academic colleagues who are devastated by the deplorables whose racism alone put Donald J. Trump in the White House.

But then I find myself with my conservative friends. Swivelling round to ensure there's not a leftie in sight, I proceed with the self-transformation required to up the chance of my acceptance. I bemoan the cosmopolitan disdain for faith, flag and family which in the end satisfy our need for roots. In the US I curse the coastal elites whose identity politics have ruptured the body politic, who eviscerate the very institutions of civil society they claim are the foundations of a healthy democratic life (for example, by threatening to punish faith schools that adhere to their historic teaching on sexuality).

Thus play I in one person many people. I inhabit a self-induced schizoid reality, and I expend a lot of energy trying to hide my hypocrisy. For I want to become a public intellectual lauded for his acute insights, but I don't want to be no-platformed. I want to make a name for myself on social media by sparking interesting conversations, but without being blocked or unfriended.

COMPETING VISIONS OF THE GOOD

Because they satisfy this need to belong, it seems obvious that our political factions are simply modern varieties of the tribes human beings have belonged to, or been raised in, throughout history. Tribes have their own heroes, saints, villains, stories, scriptures, symbols and colours. They are sites of intense emotional attachment. They confer meaning as well as secure survival. They have distinct takes on the past and visions of the future which characterize them. There are limits to the degree of internal deviance that can be tolerated. Don't our polarized political communities display these features?

Further, an intriguing feature of modernity is the way tribes come to function as 'imagined communities'. People who have never met face to face nevertheless still feel they belong to the same group, are on the same team. Group identity can survive the advent of mass society as, at the most fundamental level, we are shaped by each other, and together sustain a common creed. Members of the same tribe may never come across each other, 'yet in their minds lives the image of their communion'.[1]

Here too our political tribes fit the criteria. A liberal lumberjack in a remote part of Oregon feels closer, and is more influenced by, a New York office manager than by his next-door neighbour. A Tory pensioner settled in the leafy villas of Tunbridge Wells has more in common with a hedge-funder in Mayfair than with her own daughter.

Then there is the exclusivity of tribes. Belonging to one tribe means not belonging to another and being defined in opposition to that group. Tribes expend a lot of energy policing their boundaries and deciding who's in and who's out.

It is at this point, though, that political tribes – whether the traditional European Left, Anglo-American liberals, libertarians or social conservatives – don't fit the pattern. For this reason: *they harbour visions of the good*. That is, at their best, they traffic in ideas about the welfare of the *whole*. The values wrapped up inside the package deals have universal purchase. Those principles are about what it means to thrive as a human being and thus what it is for everyone to flourish. The vision of liberals isn't just for a world that is better for liberals. The conservative vision isn't just for a world that is better for conservatives. It may be that those principles are mistaken – identifying those principles is what this book is about. It may be that those principles are not good. But the culture wars are more than tribal blood-feuds in which the promotion of an agenda is merely the pursuit of interests. The culture wars are bitter disputes about what is true about the world. The American Right does not campaign against abortion because it wants to create an environment where the next generation of only their own group are less likely to terminate their own pregnancies. The Right genuinely believes the 'newone' is a human being and therefore that a new environment should be created for the next generation of liberal mothers too.[*] They may be wrong about that – this is a question I will take up in Chapter 4 – but if so, they are wrong about something fundamental.

---

[*] 'Newone' is the term I employ for the pre-natal human organism in my attempt to move beyond the value-laden terminology of 'foetus' or 'product of conception' by pro-choicers and 'unborn child' by pro-lifers.

This might strike you as hopelessly naïve. Do the 1 per cent really defend the value of economic freedom and pour donations into their candidates' campaigns because they're up all night worried about more resources trickling down to the middle class? Don't the National Rifle Association (NRA) just want to sell more guns? And have I not said that, by forming the package deals, the political class has conscripted fundamental moral values to further their interests? Indeed, but that's what makes it so pernicious and powerful. Political elites can form such strong coalitions with distinct groups in the electorate on single issues (and then foist the package deals upon them) because each of those groups cares so much about those single issues, and they care so much about those single issues because they provide views of the good. Therefore, in their own self-interest and desire for power, elites trade on, and masquerade as champions of, principles that are not fundamentally expressions of self-interest. Elites secure a loyal base precisely because the discrete values they package are, as visions of the good, clung to so ferociously.

Only a few months after I left Charlottesville, something terrible happened there. We had feared it was coming ever since a permit was granted for a 'Unite the Right' march to protest against the felling of statues of Confederate general Robert E. Lee from the central Charlottesville park. We feared our small, sleepy university town near the Blue Ridge Mountains would be descended upon by out-of-town white supremacists.

Still, as I refreshed my browser in London, I couldn't fathom what was unfolding. A car had ploughed down a pedestrian in the street where I used to buy my pecan pies. The delightful downtown mall I had strolled along so many evenings with my wife was full of terrorists chanting 'Blood and Soil'. The 'Lawn', the heart of the university where I taught, and where every Halloween I took my daughter to trick-or-treat undergraduates, was overrun with real monsters, torches in hand. Real, live neo-Nazis threw bottles of piss at counter-protesters in the park where my toddler used to run through splash pads in the summer.

The fall-out from 'August 12th', as it will forever be known, has been devastating. This most wonderful of towns has been put on the map for the most dreadful of reasons. The world has too often failed to recognize that James Alex Fields, Jr, the young man convicted of the murder of the pedestrian, 32-year-old Heather Heyer, lived in *Ohio*. He was not from Charlottesville. Worse, the town itself has been tragically divided over what was the right response on the day. 'Where were you on August 12th?' has become the equivalent of 'What did you do in the war, Daddy?' Those who stayed away, who did not join the counter-protest, have been sharply criticized by the activists who faced off the neo-Nazis.

What no one believes, however, is that Jason Kessler, the orchestrator of the violence, succeeded in his aim of uniting the Right in Charlottesville. My friends and neighbours who would identify as conservatives did not swell the ranks of the protesters. They were as appalled by August 12th as my liberal university colleagues.

The argument revolved around the question of blame for the universally abhorred outbreak of white supremacy, as liberals lambasted conservatives for putting in the White House a man who has energized white supremacists, while conservatives claimed the catastrophe was the inevitable outcome of identity politics – now it was the whites' turn at special pleading.

The objective of Kessler and the Alt-Right is to create a homogenous white ethno-state. 'White Countries for White People ... The end goal of the movement is to establish pure White racial states in all formerly White countries', announces the editor of the *Daily Stormer*, Andrew Anglin.[2] So the aim is not just to advance the interests of whites in the nation. Rather, as Jared Taylor elucidates the agenda, 'racial consciousness is an essential part of group identity and it should be an inevitable part of national identity as well.'[3] The vision is not just for the dominance of whites but, more alarmingly for total conquest by whites. Many in the movement do not shy away from – in fact, many are quick to reach – the shameful corollary of this heinous view: the mass deportation of non-white immigrants and the repatriation of the descendants of slaves to Africa.

Given these objectives, white supremacists constitute a movement different from Left and Right. For by definition the white supremacist message does not address all Americans. An African-American cannot convert to an Alt-Right ideology. Conservatives, by contrast, *are* taking converts. In their espousal of the moral positions in which we are interested in this book, conservatives can be seen as addressing all citizens. The values of the Right are ones that have universal purchase.

11

DISAGREEING DIFFERENTLY

Given the character of public debate, it is little wonder that recent books bewailing political tribalism conclude with calls for conciliation. 'We need to find a way to talk to each other if we are to have any chance of bridging divides', writes Amy Chua in *Political Tribes*; 'We need to allow ourselves to see our tribal adversaries as fellows ... engaged in a common enterprise.'[4] We need to break out of our parallel political universes, our actual or virtual gated communities. We need to exit the echo chambers of social media and meet each other in person – to engage with rather than demonize our liberal or conservative adversaries. The imperative is to translate promising local instances of people coming together not to dwell on their differences but to find common ground where they can work together.

According to this view – and this is the critical thing – the condition for the possibility of living together peaceably is for political factions, when it comes to their deepest principles, agreeing to disagree. Our hope lies in leaving well alone those values about which we are so conflicted.

Which seems to me the one thing we can't do. A seismic change in our mode of engagement is indeed vital – ending the vitriol and the vilification. But it can only be a necessary and not a sufficient achievement. It will not be enough. Why? Because the abolitionists did not agree to disagree. The civil rights movement did not settle for living with their differences – that would have meant capitulation, giving up on the dream of transformation. It would have entailed abandoning the aim of integration. Similarly, in our moment, agreeing

12

to disagree is the quietist option that rests content to leave things as they are. Defending our convictions in the public square – though in so different a way, rooted in the recognition of the inextinguishable humanity of one's adversary – is what it means to be committed to the good.

The defeat of tribalism hinges on our willingness to question package deals. Defying that inheritance, refusing to have the parameters of our thinking, the range of options open to us, circumscribed by ideology may itself help us to move closer towards a profoundly different political environment.

WHAT LIES AHEAD

The structure of this book reflects my attempt to break with package-deal thinking. I do this by affirming principles from across the political spectrum – three found on the Left, three on the Right. This does not mean, I should stress from the outset, that package deals are monolithic. It is critical to acknowledge that there is not one left-wing package deal spanning the Atlantic any more than there is one right-wing one, and this book is committed to distinguishing between social conservatives and libertarians, Republicans and British Conservatives, liberals and the Left.

The nineteenth-century British prime minister Benjamin Disraeli said of Lord Liverpool: 'In the conduct of public affairs his disposition was exactly the reverse of that which is characteristic of great men. He was peremptory in little questions, and great ones he left open.' In this book we will take up some of the great ones of our time: whether we should legalize assisted dying; what we should do about in-work poverty; how we are to evaluate our sexual culture; the question of gun violence; whether we pursue proposals to enhance ourselves; how we confront the collateral consequences of crime. Thinking afresh about these issues is long overdue, and it is only by escaping package deals and seeking recourse to first principles that we can do it.

1

INCLUSIVITY: SHOULD LIBERALS BACK
ASSISTED SUICIDE?

Godelieva De Troyer, a teacher from Hasselt, a small city in the Flemish region of Belgium, had suffered from severe clinical depression her whole life. The dark moods began in childhood. By 19 she was in therapy, 'confronted almost daily with the consequences of [her] childhood'. At 23 she got married, the marriage ending – two children later – in a divorce. When her ex-husband committed suicide three years later, she had to bring up her children by herself. Her relationship with them grew increasingly strained as they moved into their teenage years. Godelieva blamed herself. Tom, her son, was a 'victim of my instability', she wrote in her diary.

Things looked up in her early fifties. She found love again. Her son and his wife produced a grandchild. She was thrilled by the possibility of making up for her failures as a mother by succeeding as a grandmother. The joy was short-lived. When her boyfriend broke up with her, it precipitated another major bout of clinical depression. She withdrew once more.

It was at this point that Godelieva attended a lecture by an oncologist and professor of palliative medicine at the Free University of Brussels. Wim Distelmans was a leading proponent of a law passed in 2002 allowing euthanasia on the grounds that it would come as a 'tremendous liberation' for patients 'who have an incurable illness that causes them unbearable physical or mental suffering'. His was a broader definition of the justifiable conditions of euthanasia than simply terminal illness, and Godelieva concluded that that designation fitted her condition. 'The loneliness ...,' she said, 'no chance of a cure after forty years, years of therapy, nothing to look forward to – all this has led me to see that the only thing remaining is a dignified end of life.' She went to Distelmans himself and filed a request for a lethal injection. Three weeks later her son, who had no idea what she had been contemplating, received an email saying she had died.[1]

'The strangeness of your story put heaviness in me', says Miranda in *The Tempest*. That's what I felt when I read Godelieva's story in *The New Yorker*. In a world where so many people are living longer, better lives than ever before, how could a woman's exit look like this one? How could a woman feel she had no other option? I pored over the article, re-reading in order to try and work out where I could assign blame. I wanted to excoriate the family, but Godelieva herself didn't indulge that instinct. Then I thought about Distelmans. Should he be held responsible for putting the idea in her head? Or should he be praised for courageously, compassionately providing the way out she wanted?

In the past I've succumbed to the temptation of thinking assisted suicide a difficult but discrete moral quandary, perhaps because I had been taught it as a separate stand-alone unit in an Ethical Dilemmas class at school. It was presented as an issue about how we act in medical emergencies. But when confronted with cases from countries where assisted suicide has been legalized – stories like Godelieva's – what dawned on me was how profound a societal shift changing the law could presage. Permitting assisted suicide – regardless of whether that's the right thing to do or not, regardless of whether or not we decide it constitutes moral progress – could transform the entire way we think about ageing and deal with death.

Support for legalizing euthanasia is a position embedded in the cultural left's package deal. In this chapter I ask whether that position expresses or ignores one of the principles on the Left I find most compelling – its belief in *inclusivity*, by which I mean a commitment to identify the marginalized and protect the vulnerable. I think there is a particular historical juncture, around the turn of the twentieth century, where we see that value expressed very clearly. The Left identified and then responded to a whole class of people who found themselves radically marginalized and vulnerable. What I want to ask here is whether, given the miracle of longevity, the marginalization of the elderly is still a reality to be reckoned with. And if it is, what has that to do with this critically important decision whether to permit or continue to prohibit physician-assisted suicide?*

---

* Definitions and distinctions are complex but crucial when it comes to this vexed subject. I will, unhelpfully, use 'assisted dying', 'physician-assisted dying', 'assisted suicide' and 'euthanasia' interchangeably. The fundamental distinction, though, is between *active* and *passive* euthanasia. *Active* euthanasia denotes an

NO COUNTRY FOR OLD MEN

At the end of the nineteenth century a Victorian shipowner and merchant, Charles Booth, set out to produce the most painstaking survey of poverty ever attempted. Starting with London, Booth amassed a team of researchers and began mapping the city, colouring the East End street by street to indicate the depth of destitution. Between 1886 and 1903 he produced a whopping total of 17 volumes exposing the condition of housing, investigating various trades in order to document wage levels and employment conditions and finding that 30 per cent of London's population of one million 'souls' lived below what he was the first to call 'the poverty line'.

Immiseration was widespread, but the most desperate group Booth identified was the 'aged poor'. 'At best,' he wrote, 'for those who earn low wages, old age when it comes will probably be a time of great difficulty.' From what they were paid during their working lives, people could simply not earn enough to save. Moreover, Booth continues:

Modern conditions of industry do not favour the aged. Work is driven faster, and needs more nerve,

'active killing' – involving *either* a doctor supplying drugs to a patient who then voluntarily takes them herself ('assisted suicide' or 'assisted dying' and defined as 'manslaughter' under British law) *or, alternatively,* a patient, unable to take the drugs herself, requesting that a doctor directly terminate her life – typically by lethal injection (defined as 'murder' under British law). *Passive* euthanasia refers to a 'letting die' rather than an active killing. This breaks down into yet another distinction between the withdrawal of *treatment* (turning off a ventilator) and the withdrawal of *care* (a failure to provide food and water). The latter is, for many, seen as criminally negligent.

and its changing methods continually displace the old. The community may gain, but the old men suffer.[2]

Seniors had become, and this is a purely descriptive statement, an economic burden to society in a new way.

Liberals felt a new problem required a new solution. Previously, government had thought it was the family and community that needed to step up to deal with the poverty of the elderly. Thus laws dealt with the 'condition of the aged poor' by making it a criminal offence for children not to support their parents. For social justice liberals, however, structural economic change made this social solution seem wholly unsatisfactory: the problem was just too widespread. Now government needed to be involved. The role of the state needed to be fundamentally altered from *not* interfering in people's lives to *proactively* intervening in them to socialize risk. It was time for a guaranteed income for those beyond working age.

The Left was adamant that this prospective pension had to be national, and its reasoning was revealing. In his tract of 1907, 'Paupers and Old Age Pensions', one of the first members of the Fabian Society, Sidney Webb, made the case for why pensions must be provided by the government at a national level:

We must not have the poor old man or woman on the verge of the pensionable, refused a lodging in the parish ... dismissed from a situation or ejected from a dwelling there, in order to prevent that particular parish being *burdened* with either the whole or a part of his or her old age pension. [italics mine]

19

Webb's fear was that, if left to the local level, authorities would move people who were approaching pensionable age to another area in order to shirk their responsibility of providing for them. For Webb, a liberal commitment to social justice generated a profound concern with the marginalization of the elderly.

In the US, progressives were also driven by their concern for the marginalized elderly. In an issue of *Cosmopolitan* magazine from 1903, Edward Everett Hale published an article entitled 'Old Age Pensions'. He acknowledged an inconvenient truth: 'there is now no place in our working order for old men.'[3] In 1903 Massachusetts proposed the first old-age pension bill. In 1906 progressive social scientists founded the American Association for Labor Legislation. In 1908 the first public commission on ageing was founded, immediately carrying out the first major survey of the economic condition of the elderly. In 1909 the word 'geriatrics' was coined to designate a new social science.[4]

Despite these efforts, aversion to government interference persisted through the first three decades of the twentieth century. Attempts to establish a comprehensive pension system failed. It took the Great Depression to change minds.

One day in 1933 a family doctor named Francis Townsend saw an old woman rummaging around in a garbage can for scraps of food. Townsend had practised medicine all his life – as an army medic in the First World War; running his own practice in South Dakota; in Long

Beach, California, as a health director. But the day he saw that woman he gave up medicine to become an activist. His cause? He launched the first national campaign for a government-sponsored pension scheme. The movement was a thrillingly grassroots one. Townsend started off by writing to his local paper outlining a simple plan. Everyone over 60 should get $200 a month from the Federal Government, paid for by a 2 per cent national sales tax. He received an extraordinary response – two thousand letters a day. Republished as a pamphlet, his plan was distributed across America. A year later a thousand 'Townsend clubs' had been established. Within three years the organization had three and a half million members and twenty million signatures on petitions calling for the pension plan. And with 1936 being a presidential year, Franklin Roosevelt had to act.

Townsend was a progressive convinced the government must provide for the 'little people'. This could be the only solution to the destitution of the elderly. He wrote in his autobiography:

> From such feeble beginnings our cause has become the mightiest issue in the political history of our nation. Before our appearance on the scene, old-age pensions in America were limited to Supreme Court justices and their widows ... The little people were not organized as a pressure group, so were left out in the cold.

But now, he continued, their movement had brought to the attention of the nation and its president the demand that

> Any aging citizen whose life has been one of hard work, depressions, rearing a family, being a good citizen and a neighbour ... should be entitled to a pension when his days of physical productiveness have passed.

It was the Left's commitment to the principle of inclusivity, then – its concern for the marginalized – that led to the far-reaching reforms still in place today. Its sensitivity to the vulnerability of particular groups, and its alertness to the way power operates, led to its advocacy of the poorest older people left high and dry by industrialization. What is the case in our world, though? Is the marginalization of older people still a reality to be reckoned with? And if so, what form does it take?

MARGINALIZATION TODAY

> Aged hands are a tell-tale sign of how old you are. They're notorious for becoming wrinkly over time and displaying signs of crepiness.

A photograph to accompany this headline from the lifestyle magazine on the shelf was of a reptile – its skin leathery, gross. The implication is clear: one squirt of this skin cream will arrest the ageing process and postpone your metamorphosis.

Resist the wrinkles; avert infirmity; defer decrepitude – these were the abundant promises of the magazine shelf. 'If it's everlasting youth you seek, take action!' enthuses *New You*, proffering 30 anti-ageing tips so you can start 'rolling back the years'. Tip #29: sleep on your back because 'eliminating contact between your skin and pillow will prevent any creasing of the skin'. Then the exhortation to rearrange your face, with one doctor offering cosmetic surgery on the grounds that, 'If you're healthy enough for surgery, age doesn't mean anything.'

The celebration of film stars who don't look their age; self-help mantras promising that '70 is the New 40' if you can 'stay young in the mind'; sports presenters' incredulity that athletes could have a meaningful life past 35; the impossibility of starting a band in, say, your fifties – the cult of youth is a permanent feature of our landscape as we're fed a diet of lies.

Not every culture stokes the aspiration to grow young. In Māori culture, Kaumātua – elders both male and female – are literally afforded pride of place in the *marae* of ceremonial courtyards. This isn't just a sign of respect. There's an expectation that Kaumātua will exercise authority. When decisions have to be made regarding the allocation of resources – the deployment of *whānau*, or tribal land – it's to their wisdom the community will defer. As guardians of *tikanga*, or customs, indispensable for the transmission of tradition, it is the Kaumātua who are the masters of ceremonies. Discipline, too: the community will turn to these councils of elders when the young run amok. Teenagers who tamper with Māori *tapu*, or sacred sites, soon find themselves hauled up before the weekly gathering of elders.

Nor has modernity altered this core expectation for Kaumātua. One minister of Māori affairs explained the motivation for building community-based retirement housing. It is to ensure our elders remain the ones who 'keep our *maraes*, our communities and our lands warm with their presence'. The Māori talk of keeping their communities warm with the presence of their elderly. We prefer the language of the 'demographic time-bomb'.

Notice that it is to the Kaumātua as a distinct body that the community turns. We aren't talking about individuals' private relationships with their grandparents – a young man asking his grandfather for occasional advice, using him as a subject of 'oral testimony' for his school assignment, or a child being raised solely by her grandmother. No, what's in view here is an institution.

In Māori, the word *tipuna* refers not just to your immediate grandparents but to a community of elders. Listen to this testimony, for example:

> When I was told that an aged visitor whom I had never seen before was a tipuna to me, my heart warmed towards him. I placed him in the same category as my other tipuna who resided in the same village and had lavished affection upon me. He was a member of the family.[5]

In an Alaskan Athbaskan tribe, revolving similarly around the 'potlach' of elders, one woman told an ethnographer that her mother regularly encouraged her to seek advice from the community of elders. 'Every time I hear old people', she divulged, 'even one word will help me. When I get into a problem, the word will come back to me.'[6]

The contrast between this reverence of age and our cult of youth is shocking. Two implications follow. The first consequence of ageism is that older people become increasingly alienated from mainstream culture. Secondly, ageism translates into a marginalization that generates a sense of having become a burden.

When Alexis de Tocqueville wrote about the beginnings of democratic society in the 1830s, he saw with remarkable prescience the dramatic social transformations to come. Tocqueville believed in democracy – it was an idea whose time had come – but he anticipated the problems with a keen eye. Most notably, the levelling out of hierarchical societies would, if unchecked, lead to

each citizen cutting himself off from his fellows and withdrawing into the circle of his family and friends in such a way that he thus creates a small group of his own and willingly abandons society at large to its own devices.

The family in the industrialized West, unlike in Māori society, would contract to become what we now call the nuclear or immediate family. It would increasingly withdraw from public life. Self-condemned to a private existence, the individual begins to conceive of himself as cut off from his relatives, ancestors and descendants, his life framed now only by the present. The cost to the 'agent' in the business of his life – to young, active people cutting themselves off from their fellows – would be immense. They would lose out, to be sure. But what about the fate of elders? Those who have lost their places in larger society and now sit only at the table of their immediate family?

I added a qualification above: 'if unchecked'. The reason Tocqueville came to love America was that he saw how this process of withdrawal was in fact being checked. The withdrawal was being arrested by the fast formation of associations. 'Americans of all ages, conditions, and all dispositions constantly unite together', he observed enthusiastically.

In our time what Tocqueville feared, the withdrawal of the citizen into the circle of his family, is no longer checked. With the weakening of civil society, the thinning out of this crucial layer of intermediary association, we're back with the increasing dissolution of the wider society into the immediate family.

Those who lament the decline of vital voluntary associations have focused on the impact on the citizens, the impact on the state, on schools, on local democracy. But what of the elderly? What happens when elders are relegated to the private sphere? The loss of authority in the wider community is clearly one consequence of this marginalization. Where are the forums for intergenerational interaction, the spontaneous mutually reinforcing traffic between the young and the old? In truth, what is our reaction to older people who take an interest in children not directly related to them?

We are witnessing a sad paradox. We should be celebrating the extraordinary civilizational achievement of longevity, with more people living longer than ever before in human history. But because this is happening in the context Tocqueville feared – the withdrawal to the nuclear family – the consequence of longevity is an increasing intensity of the role of family caregiver. A 60-year-old woman, herself approaching retirement age, finds herself the only person caring for her frail mother. She would never give up the responsibility. But because there's no one else in the picture, she and her mother are becoming 'each the other world's entire'. Extended family are simply not at hand to absorb the impact of the mother's increasing needs. The daughter's caregiving is swiftly becoming a full-time job (over 50 hours a week is the usual statistic in the literature), and this is taking its toll. 'No matter how little I've slept, I have to get up in the morning', I heard from one caregiver. Caregivers are twice as likely to suffer from poor health. So, because of the collapse of wider community, what should be counted the blessing – longer retirements – often increases the curse of marginalization.

Worse, in our culture relegation *to* the family is often being followed by relegation *from* the family altogether. We know a lot about the impact of family breakdown on the young. We think less about the elderly. What is the consequence of high divorce rates as divorcees reach retirement age? What is the long-term effect of break-ups on previously unquestioned assumptions about who cares for whom towards the end of the life? A broken marriage strains the relationship between a parent and his children – how does this play out further along the line? What is the consequence of dysfunctional family structures decades later? Subsequent contact between children and now ageing parents can in many cases no longer be taken for granted. Instead, as sociologists have observed, in a high-divorce society, 'trust has to be negotiated and bargained for'. Commitment doesn't just flow automatically from a specific relationship. It is 'cumulative'. It has to be earned.[7]

We reduce the pollsters to tears. When I was working in British politics, I conducted a poll to find out whether anecdotal evidence about the isolation of older Britons was true. Many sceptics try to explain away the stark statistics – that half of people over 75 live alone – by distinguishing between solitude and loneliness. Solitude, they claim, could be compatible with living alone, whereas loneliness is not having the companionship that you want. So we conducted a Christmas telephone poll, the largest of its kind.

Here are the responses our pollsters received when they enquired about how much contact those older people had with other people on a regular basis: 'I'm 88 and I have nobody at all. I'm on my own.' 'Does the TV count? I see people on the TV all day.' 'Some days the only person I speak to is the boy in the shop when I pick up my paper.'

Most staggeringly, 40 per cent of those older people who were going to be home alone at Christmas had children living in the UK. On the biggest day of the year already isolated elders were going to be alone while their closest relatives celebrated with someone else on our small island. Relationships with their now adult sons and daughters had so deteriorated that they couldn't even manage Christmas dinner together, while the wider community could no longer provide the safety net it once did. As one gerontologist put it, 'being lonely typically represents the continuation of longstanding difficult relationships with family members and limited relationships with friends or neighbours.'[8]

This phenomenon is not confined to the UK. In the US the term 'elder orphans' has recently emerged from medical and nursing journals to designate men and women bereft of the support of nearby friends or relatives.[9] Estimates are that nearly a quarter of all elderly Americans could be 'orphans'.[10] Recent US studies suggest that family breakdown renders familial ties more tenuous.[11]

But perhaps the most potent symbol in our culture of the marginalization of the elderly are care homes. 'The outside world never comes in here,' a 90-year-old man named Jonathan told me in a rest home in Wembley, north London. To interview Jonathan in his room I had to manoeuvre my way between other residents abandoned in wheelchairs on the second-floor landing as sawdust from construction works above fell down on them. Around this traffic jam the place was a mess, and the older men and women seemed disoriented.

Jonathan fitted perfectly the changing profile of care home 'residents' – that, bluntly, they are people who are not going to be resident very long since, suffering from comorbidity, they don't have long left. With the decline of family visitors, a fact well attested to by care home managers (and in the US studies show that 60 per cent of nursing home residents do not receive visitors[12]), children from a local primary school used to be a substitute for Jonathan. Their visits made such a difference. Now they don't visit either – put off by fear at the sight of increasingly ill patients (staff putting this down to teachers' failure to prepare pupils for these encounters).

In her powerful ethnographic study *Experience of Death: An Anthropological Account* Jennifer Hockey writes: 'The literal meaning of daily life within a care home is that forty-five people have lived so long as to have outgrown their places within the outside world.' When an older person has to go into a home, she is coming to live with strangers – people she has no ties or association with. She has to shed her possessions, those things that made her home a home. And from now on she will typically become a solitary eater, reversing the civilizational step whereby the human need for regular fuel became a chance to affirm sociality by eating together. Homes may be run by extraordinary overworked, underpaid care workers, but they still constitute for Hockey 'institutionalized marginality', 'a virtual exile from society', 'zones of social abandonment', a last resort for those who await death and have 'toppled over the edge of the social map',[13] 'zones of social abandonment'. Jokes, as always, Hockey finds particularly revealing. When residents see staff with empty rubbish bags they will often joke, 'you might as well put me in there'. Hockey writes: 'residents' use of rubbish as a metaphor for themselves, though made oblique through humor, nonetheless constitutes a succinct and powerful statement about their marginalized social status, as well as their fragile physical state.'

The marginalization, then, goes all the way down. It began with marginalization from a position of authority in wider society, then became a withdrawal to the stifling circle of the immediate family, then alienation from the family itself and the subsequent isolation, ending with banishment to care homes. The irony is unavoidable: a society that prizes living longer is uncomfortable with old age and the people who attain it.

But what does this all amount to? In short, the objective reality of marginalization is experienced subjectively as a deep sense of being a burden. Let's look at what's always the giveaway: money.

WHERE THERE'S A WILL THERE ARE RELATIVES

In Charles Dickens's great novel of 1843, *Martin Chuzzlewit*, the health of old Martin is failing. He is a rich man, a very rich man. But since he has no living children, as soon as his relatives hear his strength is waning they all crawl out of the woodwork. Distant family members suddenly appear at the Blue Dragon, the inn where the ill, grouchy old patriarch Martin has taken a room. Chuzzlewit's snivelling, sycophantic cousin Mr Pecksniff turns up at the bedside. His stealthy nephew Mr Chevy Slyme, unable to get into the room itself, is forced literally to peek through the keyhole. Mrs Spottletoe, the old man's niece and, we are told, 'a favourite once', has turned up downstairs, while Martin's twin brother, Anthony, and his son Jonas 'have got wind of it' too, swooping in like vultures to try and get their hands on Martin's estate. Learning of his competitors, Pecksniff – the most notorious hypocrite in English literature – cries out: 'the rapacity of these people is absolutely frightful ... Oh, Mammon. Mammon!'

But the old man is not oblivious to what's going on. When Pecksniff first addresses him as 'Good cousin', Martin Chuzzlewit thunders:

There! His very first words! In his very first words he asserts his relationship! I knew he would: they all do! Near or distant, blood or water, it's all one. Ugh!

Martin Chuzzlewit's family compete to get one over on him. But Martin sees what they're doing. Because what they are doing is sufficiently overt to him.

In our world, when it comes to money and inheritance, older people don't see what we're doing, and that's because *we* don't see what we're doing. For, quite simply, our attitude to capital is out of date, belonging to a world where people didn't live as long with such high care costs – we can't abide the idea of our parents' or grandparents' capital being eaten up by their care costs.

One of the great vote-winners for politicians has been those frequently made promises to find a solution to this problem. Twenty years ago, the British prime minister

Tony Blair declared, 'I don't want our children brought up in a country where the only way pensioners can get long-term care is by selling their home.' Across the West policy units, think-tanks, departments of state, institutes, universities, the brightest minds and boldest thinkers have wrestled with the question of how to preserve capital from the ravages of care costs. But few of these geniuses or gerontologists have ever questioned the premise that capital is sacrosanct and the inheritances of the younger generation theirs by right.

Old Martin Chuzzlewit saw the pressure he was being put under by his relatives. We, the relatives, don't even see the pressure our cultural expectations put our parents and grandparents under. The result is an older generation that, without anyone ever having said anything explicit to them, has picked up from the larger culture a reluctance to use their money to pay for their care. There is, of course, something perennial about this, something natural about wanting to hand on wealth to your children. But in our time, when people are living longer than ever before, hasn't it become anachronistic to assume that their capital must be our inheritance?

Historically, the Left has always been acutely sensitive to the dynamics of power. The famous French postmodern theorist Michel Foucault was profoundly alert to ways in which power is dispersed through society. For people to be controlled they don't need an evil genius sending out members of his secret police to enforce the law. Far more efficiently, if certain norms can become internalized, people will act within those norms. And attitude to capital is a prime example of this. A norm has taken hold in the culture – manifest in the strong aversion to using equity to pay for care – which has inculcated a sense that eventually the elderly are using up their kids' inheritance, that they're a drain on resources. Because someone doesn't have to be told he's a burden to begin to believe he is one. And internalizing an out-of-date norm leaves people not enjoying every moment of later life but, rather, feeling they are a burden.

UNDER PRESSURE

Inclusivity, then – a commitment to protect the vulnerable and identify the marginalized – is central to the Left's moral vision. And in our world marginalization is subjectively experienced by older people feeling themselves a burden to society. The question that faces us now is how the introduction of assisted dying would play in this cultural context.

The conditions are clearly spelt out. They are there for everyone to see. Quite explicit. The law permitting assisted dying – first introduced in Oregon, serving now as a template for other American states and a model for British proposals – is supposed to include the strictest of stipulations. The terminally ill patient requesting lethal medication must have 'voluntarily expressed his or her wish to die' and 'is not being coerced to sign the request'.[14] How could there even be a question, then, that people will be under pressure to shorten their lives, that vulnerable older men and women will be at risk? Where is the room for abuse?

The answer hinges on the view of power examined above. Power is not always synonymous with physical force. Power can be dispersed when certain norms are internalized. Someone wants to end their life because somewhere along the way they have picked up from wider society, or specifically from their families, a sense that they are a burden. Are we going to deny they are under pressure, that they are being unduly influenced by external forces? A son watching his inheritance being exhausted on hospice fees is not going to wheel his father into a doctor's office with a gun to his father's head. That doesn't mean that what's going on may not be profoundly coercive. Coercion can take subtle forms, forms that are not going to be discernible at the precise moment someone issues their request to die.

Consider another way pressure can be exerted. At first sight, it seems odd to think that it can be burdensome to have **more** options. But as the philosopher David Velleman argues, this could be precisely what would happen if the euthanasia option is put on the table. For in the case of the terminally ill or chronically disabled the option of assisted suicide 'will deny them the possibility of staying alive by default'. What does Velleman mean by that?

> Once a person is given the choice between life and death, he will rightly be perceived as the agent of his own survival. Whereas his existence is ordinarily viewed as a given for him – as a fixed condition with which he must cope – formally offering him the option of euthanasia will cause his existence thereafter to be viewed as his doing.[15]

Doing nothing, simply carrying on – the sheer prolongation of your life – will come to be seen as an active choice, and therefore a choice that requires justification. You could choose to be assisted to die. You could choose to refuse. But the game has changed. Someone's existence will become their responsibility in a new way. The onus will be on the people who are ill to explain why they are not availing themselves of the option to die with assistance.

Imagine an older man in a doctor's waiting room who's just been given a diagnosis of Stage 4 cancer. He is left reeling. He didn't expect a diagnosis this dreadful. Nothing before in his life has prepared him for how to deal with this. At this point he is handed two brochures. One offers 'dignity in dying' – a painless, inexpensive, 'humane' death. The other brochure offers hospice care – by implication the undignified, inhumane option. Because assisted dying has become as viable an option as hospice care, because they are two equal alternatives, now the man, on the most difficult day of his life, has to make a case to himself why more months of life in a hospice are worth living and paying for.

We can envisage that man feeling pressure from another direction too. In a recent article in the *New England Journal of Medicine*, a group of doctors have called for Canada to remove clinical obstacles to organ donation from men and women who have sought voluntary euthanasia. At present the 'dead donor rule' stipulates that organs cannot be removed until the person has been declared dead – typically between two and ten minutes after the onset of pulselessness.[16] The problem is that such a delay can compromise the quality and limit the number of retrievable organs. And so, the doctors propose, patients should be able to choose to be anaesthetized for a period before their death while their organs are procured.

The spectre of doctors extracting organs from the living is haunting on its own. But the central point is that we can easily imagine an additional onus being placed on the terminally ill. If a man is troubled by the thought that it would be more selfless to die, rather than needlessly to prolong his life, how much more selfless would it be, he might think, to request help to end his life in order to donate his organs? The impulse to altruism could become a duty to die. The possibility of choosing to die and donating your organs could so easily become choosing to die *in order to* donate your organs.

WHY SOME SLOPES ARE SLIPPERY

My argument, then, is this: that a concern for the most marginalized elderly, an application in this context of the principle of inclusivity, should eventuate in opposition to assisted dying. That is because the most vulnerable, isolated, older people could be pressured to relieve their family and society of the burden they believe they have become.

In saying this, the objection will be that I have relied on a 'slippery slope' argument. That's because I *have* relied on a slippery slope argument. The reason I have done so is because I believe a sense of history, even recent history, yields the conclusion that some slopes are slippery.[17]

What the Benelux experience demonstrates, I think, is that as soon as euthanasia is legalized, strictly circumscribed criteria quickly become viewed as discriminatory. One person's safeguards become another's barriers to entry. So, first off, a 'candidate' for assisted dying has to be terminally ill and judged as having at most six months to live. That is the safeguard. But why six months? Does that not discriminate against those with seven months to live? And what about those who are *chronically* ill? Or, if the law is extended to cover those suffering from severe physical ill-health, why does that not discriminate against those with mental health conditions? As we saw at the beginning of the chapter in the tragic case of Godelieva De Troyer, depression now counts as a terminal illness in Belgium, while *The New Yorker* also reported recently on a tragic case of a transgender person who, after a sex change, looked in the mirror and 'saw a monster' and then opted for assisted suicide.

Indeed, in Anglo-Saxon countries the debate over the criteria is in many places as fierce as the debate of legalizing euthanasia even in the most narrowly circumscribed range of cases – even where euthanasia has not been legalized. *The Economist* recently managed to slide down the slippery slope in the course of its own 1,200-word leader.[18] It began by attacking slippery slope arguments. It ended by complaining that 'Oregon's law covers only conditions that are terminal. That is too rigid ... doctor-assisted dying on the grounds of mental suffering should [also] be allowed.'

The criteria could prove one such slippery slope. Consent could prove another. As I write today, a story has come in from Canada about Audrey Parker, 57, a make-up artist suffering from cancer. Audrey has been preparing what she calls her 'beautiful death'. Having meticulously choreographed her final days, written her own obituary, these plans were upended by her realization she might not, given the nature of her illness, be fully lucid at the time of death and thus able to satisfy the requirements of the current law. For this reason she decided to commit suicide months before she had previously intended to die.

So as soon as assisted dying is legalized, pressure is exerted on a government to follow the lead of the Benelux countries and relax the legal insistence on consent at the time of death. Campaigners are now saying people should be allowed to plan their deaths ahead of time, that the law shouldn't demand competency at the precise moment of death. Once more, one person's safeguards have become another's barrier to entry, because those with illnesses that happen to allow for the requisite lucidity at the moment of death are eligible, but those with illnesses that don't allow for that are not. How is that distinction not arbitrary, unfair and thus discriminatory? Thus, the campaign groups are fighting the next frontier of the debate: they are on to the next battleground, advocating the legitimacy of accepting advance directives. The campaigning organization Dignity in Dying said: '[Audrey] was worried ... that if she waited too long, she would lose capacity and then she would be completely denied the right to have an assisted death.'

Wild speculation is rooted in sober reality. Some slopes are slippery, some descents inevitable.

Another slope that must be considered is how euthanasia could move from being initially a rare, exceptional option to being normalized as a widespread practice and institution in the culture which guides action, sets expectation, holds sway in people's minds and moves us towards certain outcomes.

The campaign to legalize euthanasia is typically formulated in liberal terms as a 'right to die'. This constitutes a 'negative right' – a right construed as a zone of freedom from government interference. Some people simply desire the freedom to arrange privately for their family doctor to help them die painlessly at the time of their choosing. What also seems important is thinking about the implication of a right to die shifting from a negative right to a positive right – that is, one that imposes a duty on the government to assist dying.* What will happen if euthanasia, as in some places already, becomes something you can get on the state? The case will be that if I am infirm and I try and die by my own hand, I could fail, preventing me from exercising my right to decide the timing and circumstances of my death. Doctors, however, have expertise to help me die 'successfully'. Therefore, I have the right to assistance from physicians. Thus the danger of government provision of assistance at the end of life is that it becomes a normal item on the menu of the state's services. Under the banner of

---

* The distinction between negative and positive rights is much contested in political philosophy. Historically, 'negative rights' have referred to the basic freedoms that liberal philosophers since John Locke derive from our basic equality – the right to property, the right not to be tortured, the right to a fair trial, the right to free speech. These rights are called 'negative' because they entail external forces *not* interfering with you. Rights are construed as immunities, zones of freedom designating no-go areas for government. Yet when people talk about rights they also invoke – as does the UN Declaration – the right to education, or healthcare or employment. These rights don't quite line up with the right to property or free speech. Why? Because their successful performance requires someone else to do something for you rather than refrain from action. The corresponding obligation, the duty correlate to the right, involves active assistance. The terminology of 'positive rights' reflects this. Thus debates about health care are controversial because if it can be said I have a positive right to it, the government has a duty to provide it. The government isn't just required to leave you alone but is summoned to act.

distributive justice, assisted suicide becomes not just an option but a culture, creating yet more pressure.

THE RELIEF OF SUFFERING?

Noel Conway was a walker. A British sociology professor, he moved to Shropshire – 'one of the hidden glories of the UK' – in 1976.[19] It proved an idyllic home for an active man. He and his wife, Carol, he says, 'have walked every inch of the Shropshire Hills with our children and Snowdonia is our backyard'. Nor were his adventures limited to the UK. He and Carol have climbed glaciers in the Alps, cycled along the Danube and skied through the Milky Way system between France and Italy.

A diagnosis of motor neurone disease (MND) is devastating for anyone, but there is a particular cruelty about it for so active a man. Future trips were cancelled with the onset of back pain. 'For Carol and I, it signalled the end of all our plans for the future.' Today Noel relies on a hoist to get in and out bed, he is on a ventilator for 20 hours a day and he feels 'entombed'. This is how he has reflected on his state of mind:

> I felt like a condemned man awaiting execution on a date yet to be determined. My immediate response was to get it over with as quickly as possible. I became aware of how agonising it must be to be someone on death row for years and years not knowing when the order will come.

To mitigate this sense of uncertainty and dread, Noel has campaigned for a change in the law which would allow him to receive medical assistance to die. He has always been in control of his life. Now he wants to be in control of his death: to die without suffering, in the manner of his choosing, on his own terms and at the right time. 'I can't change what's going to happen,' he says; 'I am going to die anyway.'

The objection to my argument will be that the Left is indeed committed to the principle of inclusivity; it is just that the candidate group for inclusion are the terminally ill, like Noel Conway, who know their minds and are desperate to die. *They* are the marginalized; *they* are the vulnerable. (Thus, the pervasive language of 'mercy killing'.) How should we respond to this powerful counter? Do we have to settle for a stark choice between favouring the interests of the terminally ill who want to die, or favouring the interests of older people who could be put under pressure to hasten their deaths?

It might appear so: that we are unable to resist the kind of utilitarian head-count approach that would see us deciding to legalize assisted dying if the number of the former group outstripped the latter. But I think there is something more foundational to say. It is that, if we define inclusivity as 'protecting the vulnerable', it seems strange to say that we are protecting the terminally ill by assisting their deaths. Perhaps it could be said that we would be protecting Noel Conway from the ravages of illness. But in that case would not, as many have argued, the most appropriate *medical* response to the tragedy of terminal illness be the provision of hospice care?

41

I WANT TO BURDEN MY LOVED ONES

In a beautiful essay entitled 'I Want To Burden My Loved Ones', the ethicist Gilbert Meilaender wrote this, and it is worth quoting at length:

> Is this not in large measure what it means to belong to a family: to burden each other – and to find, almost miraculously, that others are willing, even happy, to carry such burdens? Families would not have the significance they do for us if they did not, in fact, give us a claim upon each other. At least in this sphere of life we do not come together as autonomous individuals freely contracting with each other. We simply find ourselves thrown together and asked to share the burdens of life while learning to care for each other. We may often resent such claims on our time and energies. We did not, after all, consent to them ... It is, therefore, understandable that we sometimes chafe under these burdens. If, however, we also go on to reject them, we cease to live in the kind of moral community that deserves to be called a family. Here more than in any other sphere of life we are presented with unwanted and unexpected interruptions to our plans and projects. I do not like such interruptions any more than the next person. But it is still true that morality consists in large part in learning to deal with the unwanted and unexpected interruptions to our plans. I have tried, subject to my limits and weaknesses, to teach that lesson to my children. Perhaps I will teach it best when I am a burden to them in my dying.[20]

To say it's a tragedy when older people come to see themselves as a burden could mean two things. First, it could mean many older people are simply mistaken. They think they are burdens when in fact they are not. They are not a drain on resources but in fact have so much to contribute, are repositories of untapped wisdom (as they are perceived in the more traditional societies we examined earlier). But the tragedy could refer to something else. An alternative meaning would concede that many older people have in fact become a burden, but would insist that being a burden does not constitute a pathology. Differently put, only if autonomy is valorized and equated with 'normal' human functioning, can ageing be understood as something that has gone wrong.

What I have tried to argue in this chapter is that because the threat (that being a burden be interpreted as a pathology) is a constant one, an affirmation of the principle of inclusivity should entail that we oppose legalizing assisted dying. The room for abuse is too broad, the risk too great. We can perhaps apply Meilaender's description of a supportive family also to describe a truly inclusive society, one that cares for the vulnerable rather than abandoning them to an early death: 'We simply find ourselves thrown together and asked to share the burdens of life while learning to care for each other.'

2

FAMILY VALUES: WHY SOCIAL CONSERVATIVES SHOULD RAISE WAGES

I don't understand how I can work at two jobs and not have enough money to put food in the house. We need to be able to live.

Mona Lee lives in Kansas City and works half the day at McDonald's and the other half at Sonic, another fast-food restaurant. Her story was profiled as part of a unique exhibition entitled 'I, Too, Am America'. In collaboration with a photojournalist, she and 15 other fast-food workers in Kansas City shot more than 4,000 photos on their mobile phones, documenting what their lives are like at work and at home – their errands, their needs, their neighbourhoods, their families. The images are startling: back-of-the-envelope budget calculations, empty refrigerators, barely furnished rooms, beds on floors, boarded-up homes, bags of groceries from soup kitchens, overcrowded houses. ('Three generations, one room' reads the title of one photo.[1])

The purpose of the project, according to another exhibitor, Zoe Abbey, 32, is to educate the public: 'It's about letting them know how we live. We're not that different from you. We want to live and we want to thrive.' A key part of this, Zoe says, is correcting the stereotype that 'all fast-food workers are teenagers who live with their parents and don't have responsibilities'.[2] (According to the Bureau of Labor Statistics, the median age of women working in the fast-food industry is exactly Abbey's age.[3])

For Melinda Robinson, 38, the message to get across is the precariousness of her existence: 'I want you to understand what it's like to live in poverty, not being able to pay for the necessities we need.' Although both she and her husband work, they have fallen behind on the rent and had their electricity cut off. Both parents are holding down jobs, yet they still struggle to provide for the children, who bounce on a dirty sofa in her proudest picture.[4]

———

I felt uncomfortable about it, to be truthful – about our message. I was working at a political 'think-tank' in London. Our role in the plethora of lobbying groups that constitute the 'Westminster village' was to feed in policy ideas to government about how to tackle the kind of poverty in which Mona, Zoe and Melinda are ensnared. What I felt ambivalent about was the line we were taking on families. 'We' were really sticking our necks out. Children fare best when raised by two married parents, we were claiming. That is the context in which children are most likely to thrive. For years no one had dared say that in British politics, for fear of appearing paternalistic or, worse, seeming to disparage the achievements of single parents, or unmarried ones. Thus we made every effort to qualify our claim. We insisted that you don't have to downplay the heroism of lone mothers and fathers in order to maintain the view that, in terms of the model we should be aiming at, marriage makes a material difference. But, in the end, there was no shying away from the fact we were going out on a limb.

It wasn't this normative claim I was in two minds about, however. I had come to find it compelling (see more below). What I was feeling increasingly disconcerted by was Part II of our thesis – the corollary we were thereby defending. Faced with the fact that family breakdown is concentrated amongst the poorest, we were concluding that it was primarily a lack of commitment to marriage that was the problem. But the more I engaged with the issue, the more it seemed that drawing this conclusion hid from view other major factors that account for the fate of the most destitute families. Obvious things like not having enough money. I wondered why we were so determined to deny these material factors.

The answer, I can see with the benefit of hindsight, is that we had subscribed to a package deal. Tacked onto our family values were another set of political-economic positions, and the two approaches seemed impossible to square. Once again, principles I found expressed in one part of the package – I'll call them 'family values' – I found ignored in another. Differently put, if the poverty of working families cannot simply be put down to cultural factors, what responses to poverty should we expect from conservatives who extol family values?

THE TRUE ORIGIN OF SOCIETY

Their manifestos are unwavering: 'The family is something "conservatives believe in and work to

46

conserve".'[5] 'The family is society's central core of energy.'[6] Their politicians are agreed: 'We must strengthen the family, because it is the family that has the greatest bearing on our future.' 'Families are the most important institution in our society. We have to do everything in our power to strengthen them.'[7] It is the preoccupation of the columnists: 'Families with children are the core around which American communities must be organized ... the engine that makes American communities work.' And the centre-right think-tanks are of one voice. The American Heritage Foundation describes the family as 'the true origin of society'.[8] And the stated mission of the enormously influential Focus on the Family organization is 'to defend the God-ordained institution of the family'.[9]

We all know that social conservatives care deeply about the family. But, on the face of it, why isn't that a trivial claim? Who doesn't care about the family? Who would deny that family matters: that people bereft of families suffer a predicament and that children belong in families? It's not as if liberals pine for Plato's *Republic* or for ancient Sparta, where children were taken from their families and brought up by the state. Nor would they like to have another go at a modern equivalent – Pol Pot's communism on speed. During the horrific regime of the Khmer Rouge, Pol Pot attempted again to realize Plato's fantasy and give society a complete makeover by abolishing the family. Children were separated from their parents and brought up in communes where they called every adult 'parent'.

No, the family remains our shared ideal. It is our primary site of belonging. It is where we wake up and find ourselves in the world. It is where we care for and bear one another up. It is the primary site of reciprocity, give-and-take over time. It is the venue where we grow up and gain confidence and are nurtured, where we are treated as people so we can become people. It is often said, with a sigh, that you don't choose your family. But there's a blessing and not a curse in that, for your family don't choose you either, and so unconditional love is built into the very institution.

Families don't always function this way, of course, but we lament it when they don't because we still expect them to, and liberals participate in this lamentation no less than conservatives. Nor is it as if liberals are blind to the realities social services deal with every day – the tragedies of girls and boys constantly on the move between parents, never knowing how long their dresses and trousers will hang in the wardrobes, not knowing whether their suitcases will or will not gather dust under their new beds. Children subjected to multiple parental partnerships – born to single mothers who marry their fathers, then divorce, marry again, divorce again.

All of which is to say that social conservatives don't have a monopoly on concerns about the family. So why is it that when we hear the phrase 'family values' we associate it with conservatives? The answer has something to do with ideals, diagnosis and solutions. It has something to do with marriage. Social conservatives contest what they see as liberals' indifference to *family structure*. They believe deeply that the family structure that works out best for children is two parents who stay together, and that the best chance of staying together lies in marriage.

Social conservatives have a particular take on the ideal. They also have a distinct view of the compromise.

They don't assume the ideal will always be perfectly realized. Instead, they have a particular answer to the question: when things aren't working out in a marriage, what is the next best thing? What form should the non-ideal relational situation take? What should be the compromise? How much better is a rocky marriage, where couples stay together, than divorce? How much better is staying together despite deep difficulties than breaking up? When the ideal is not being realized, when the marriage is not faring well, what to do? Is lone parenthood to be preferred to struggling marriages? Or is lone parenthood a predicament to be avoided at all costs?

Conservatives maintain the latter because of their firm convictions about alternative outcomes for children. The results are in, they say. Children from intact families, where unhappy parents stay together, tend to do better in school and in society at large. While, with crucial exceptions like in cases of psychological and physical abuse, when family breakdown is the norm, children fare worse than they do in homes where parents struggle through. Children who suffer a series of transitions and upheavals in the home have more difficulties than those raised in stable two-parent families.[10] Children from broken homes may face the merry-go-round of frequently damaging step-parent relationships. They are more likely to act up in class at a young age, have sexual intercourse earlier or get into trouble with the law.

Zadie Smith's novel *On Beauty* centres on the deterioration of a 30-year marriage between Kiki and

Howard Belsey. At one particularly poignant moment, in the immediate aftermath of passionate lovemaking, Kiki confronts her husband:

> I'm not going to be getting any *thinner* or any *younger* ... and I want to be with somebody who can still *see me in here*. I'm still *in* here. And I don't want to be *resented* or *despised* for changing ... I'd rather be alone. I don't want someone to have *contempt* for who I've become. I've watched *you* become too. And I feel like I've done my best to honour the past, and what you were and what you are now – but you want something more than that, something new. I can't *be* new. Baby, we've had a good run. ... Thirty years – almost all of them *really happy*. That's a lifetime, it's incredible. Most people don't get that. But maybe this is just over, you know? Maybe it's over ...[11]

It is doubtful that Howard entered his marriage envisaging a divorce. But what he doesn't appreciate about marriage is that the experience of change is integral to it. For your spouse to change over time – to become different from the person you've married – should be the normal expectation for those starting out, not the excuse for calling things off even after 'a good run'.

TEETERING ON THE EDGE

For social conservatives, then, 'family values' refer to a specific vision about human flourishing – one that centres on family structure. Marriage is the form of life given for couples to live and children to come of age.

Convinced of this, the concentration of family breakdown among the poorest constitutes a profound crisis. The collapse of marriage – in the form of either divorce or unmarried partners splitting up – is for social conservatives a defining tragedy of our time. In the UK, poverty levels for children growing up in lone-parent families are almost double those of children living in two-parent families.[12]

Bereft of a second income, life as a lone parent can be brutal. The British Joseph Rowntree Foundation recently published a longitudinal study of 15 lone mothers who had been interviewed regularly over a period of 14 to 15 years.[13] It provides a devastating window onto the impact of family breakdown on women in low-income work. Many gave examples of how living within their means meant personally going without; others told tales of their not having enough, when their children grew up, to provide a buffer to survive emergencies.

After she first separated, Wendy had spent three years on benefits. But she landed a job at her first interview. Yet after 14 years working, and two years studying part-time at a university, she still felt nowhere near secure. The value of her wage was massively diminished, being the sole income for her family. She expressed concerns about money and debts. 'My financial circumstances are always just teetering on the edge.'

Other women spoke of the emotional cost of bearing the burden of keeping the money coming in. They rued the time they had lost with their children. One woman remarked: 'I fitted it in but I'm sure there were times when, you know, I feel I've missed out with them and they maybe felt they've missed out with me a bit because … but then I think they always saw, because I was the sole provider, I didn't really have an option.' Studies such as this show that in one way it is clearly true to say that family breakdown causes poverty. When family breakdown entails the loss of a second income, and a previous partner's alimony payments are insufficient, parent and child will be materially worse off. No, the controversy over the relationship between family breakdown and poverty lies elsewhere. The controversy is over what causes family breakdown in the first place. Are the reasons financial, or are they fundamentally cultural: that is, a lack of commitment to marriage – either to getting or to staying married?

The Right's focus on the latter, on the cultural issues, is due in large part to a certain story about the collapse of marriage in society at large in the second half of the twentieth century. An acceleration of the breakdown of traditional lifelong marriage was 'the single most significant identifiable consequence of the developments of the sixties'.[14] A profound change to the deep structures of culture, the new individualism of the post-war generation, gave rise to what sociologist Barbara Whitehead termed 'expressive divorce'. Whereas in the past spouses might have judged the success of their marriage on how well they were doing financially, or how well their children were doing overall, now they were more likely to take stock based on whether their personal needs and desires were being met. Divorce, Whitehead put it, held out the chance to 'make oneself over from the inside out, to refurbish and express the inner self'.[15] Writ large, in terms of societal attitudes, this shift in focus onto individual satisfaction resulted in a tendency to give others greater latitude to leave unhappy relationships.[16]

This radical shift in attitudes occurred first among elites. Emphasizing this fact is key to the conservative story, suggesting that it was not financial pressures that doubled divorce rates from 1960 to 1980.[17] The sexual revolution, to which we will turn our attention more fully in the next chapter, erupted on college campuses. The swinging '70s was a middle-class phenomenon. It was the educated who were advocating and first enacting new norms.

What happens next is cultural trickle-down, the Right insist – the unleashing of detrimental elite norms among the most deprived. Crudely, the poorest catch up. But what we then see post-1980 is that the very agents of marriage's destruction flock back to it. Committed relationships stabilize among the elite but go into free fall among the poor. Today the 'divorce divide' in America sees college-educated married couples about half as likely to divorce as the less educated.[18]

Now, here's the point of the story: because a lamentable cultural change results in the nosedive of marriage among the elite a generation ago – that is, the rise of expressive individualism and concomitant lack of commitment to marriage – the Right assumes that it is the persistence of those cultural issues among the poor today that explains the levels of family breakdown we are seeing. This is the 'culture of poverty' thesis, and the next section is dedicated to questioning it.

FAMILIES UNDER FIRE

Social scientists speak of the 'orientations' that develop among those living in deprivation, most significantly a concern with the present and not the future. A person's sense of her lack of control over her circumstances can lead to a passive acceptance of events that displaces the ability to take the initiative. And marriage and family suffer because a commitment to marriage is rooted in an orientation to the future and not just the present.

A recent study by psychologists Sendhil Mullainathan and Eldar Shafir explores how scarcity, defined as the lack of resources to do what you need to do (including time, critically, and not just money), dramatically impairs judgement.[19] Decision-making among both groups is equally compromised when deprived of time. It affects our intellectual bandwidth – a range of capacities ranging from our IQ and computational aptitude to impulse control and ability to keep to commitments. 'When we function under scarcity,' the study finds, 'we represent, manage and deal with problems differently.'[20] Not well, that is. Pressure does not focus the mind like we think it might, improving job performance. Therefore, the surroundings and educational background of the executive and the low-wage worker may be radically different, but the end behaviour is similar. The difference is, however, that the rich have an option. The executive can decide to work less. Often the poorest don't have that luxury; they can't simply eradicate all of the external factors that tax their bandwidth. Thus, scarcity can have a profound impact on marriage and the family.

In his book *Our Kids: The American Dream in Crisis*, the leading sociologist Robert Putnam focuses on the harrowing story of a teenager called Kayla.[21] Kayla hails from Bend, Oregon – a town segregated on class lines between long-term residents working in real estate (as well as affluent newcomers) and unskilled labourers from a dying timber industry who can only find work in low-wage sectors. Kayla's parents, Joe and Darleen ('low-wage refugees from disastrous first marriages'), met at Pizza Hut. Now divorced, they look back on their relationship: 'We probably didn't know each other ... We wasn't really stable. I kept thinking "Okay, we're just barely making ends meet now. Now we got a baby on the way."' They were dirt poor, living a hand-to-mouth existence in a trailer, on the income from Joe's transient jobs as cook, construction worker and gas station attendant.

For Kayla, the result was a life of radical insecurity, deprivation and loss. She missed out on what other children have. On her tenth birthday, she recalled,

> I couldn't have a cake or anything like that because we were struggling so bad. My dad said, 'We don't really have the money for it. We're going to do it in May or June.' I was like 'Oh, okay.' I was pretty sad about it, but I was like 'whatever'.

After Darleen fled the family, living an itinerant life with a new boyfriend in which she ended up homeless, Kayla was deeply scarred, her problems compounded by her issues with her new stepmother, who would 'treat her sons and daughter like royalty ... [while] I was kind of like the peasant of them all'. She has come to hate school – 'she doesn't associate with the kids', a school social worker once said, 'she just goes off by herself and sits'. Asked how she now feels about the onset of adulthood, she has one great fear – 'kind of having my life go downhill ... everything kind of falling apart'.

It's difficult to conclude that it is purely expressive individualism that is to blame for the break-up that has so affected Kayla's life. Joe and Darleen aren't a Bay area couple who have casually decided to go their separate ways. Kayla blames her mother, certainly, but financial hardship has clearly exerted huge pressure on her relationship. Living on the edge of destitution is no formula for a flourishing marriage.

Because of the radical extent to which financial hardship puts pressure on relationships, it is unsurprising how damaging the rise of precarious work has been for the family.

Take the new scheduling technology that Starbucks and many other chains have developed. 'It's like magic,' says Charles DeWitt, in charge of business development for the firm that provides the technology.[22] The software is magical because it can offer employers live information so they can determine when workers are needed and when they aren't. Retailers can bring in more workers ahead of a big delivery. It can send workers home when sales are slowing. It can flex hours to meet its needs.

The impact on the family is illustrated well by the case of Jannette Navarro, 22, a Starbucks barista from San Diego, California. Jannette was working hard to make things happen in her life.[23] The daughter of a drug addict and an absentee father, she was determined to break the cycle of dysfunction. Having just come off benefits, she secured her job at Starbucks by sheer persistence, turning up again and again asking for work.

She was doing everything to overcome the obstacles life had thrown in her path.

But the obstacle she found insurmountable was not of her own making. It was the precarious nature of her employment. First, she rarely learned about her schedule before the start of the working week, and was given little advance notice of whether her shift was going to be at dawn or at dusk, whether she'd be opening or closing up the shop. Second, and just as bad, she didn't know how many hours she was going to get per week – a nightmare for budgeting. Work meant always being available, always on call, always disruptable.

The impact on her parenting has been immense. The most basic requirements of bringing up her four-year-old child were constantly under threat. 'You're waiting on your job to control your life,' she said, 'from how much sleep Gavin will get to what groceries I'll be able to buy this month.' Sometimes she had to wake Gavin before five in the morning because of her schedule. All the things that we know are essential to the stability of the home – routine, bedtime rituals, homework monitoring, family mealtimes, let alone quality time – were compromised.

Meanwhile, erratic hours wreaked havoc on her relationships. She and her partner, Nick (Gavin is the son of a previous partner), were trying to build a new family together. Nick increasingly became Gavin's surrogate father, and the two of them pooled their resources to manage her schedule. 'Things were finally starting to come into order,' she said. But eventually Nick started to feel the strain: 'I've bitten off more than I can chew,' he said, unable to cope with the chaos of her life. Eventually Jannette and Gavin left Nick's house with no place to live.

WHEN WORK ISN'T ENOUGH

So, money matters. Financial pressure affects families. Scarcity taxes bandwidth and erodes agency. Low wages stress marriages. Poverty does not just simply result from family breakdown but often causes it.

We are now in a position to see how it is the denial of this reality – that is, 'the culture of poverty' thesis – which sustains the right-wing package deal. For if insufficient material resources aren't a fundamental problem for the poorest, you don't have to question the compatibility of family values with many of the Right's political-economic positions. You can screen off concerns about the kind of capitalism we live with today. You can mute those nagging questions. For if it's purely people's lack of commitment that causes the family breakdown so clearly associated with poverty, then deal with that. Contend with the cultural issues. If, on the other hand, not having enough money really does threaten marriage, then you need to reckon with reasons why the economy is failing the poorest families.

Recall the situations of Mona, and Zoe and Melinda, the contributors to the 'I, Too, Am America' photography exhibition. Strivers not shirkers, struggling not straggling, these women are not outliers but representative of a growing group of the population whose wages are insufficient to sustain a life for themselves and their children.

The rise of the working poor is a phenomenon to which people are increasingly alert.[24] The causes are deep-rooted. The severing of the pay of the poor from the growth of the economy is one of the defining crises of a generation. In the US, since 1979, while the wages of the top 10 per cent have rocketed, wages for the bottom 10 per cent have flat-lined, making it the longest period of stagnation since the 1860s.[25]

One story is that the stagnation in wage growth is the natural outcome of market forces. On this account, the rise of in-work poverty is owing to the ineluctable forces of globalization and technology. The market has rewarded those with greater skills and education. The rise of automation and cheap off-shore labour has both destroyed many jobs in tradable goods sectors and depressed the wages of those who have remained in post, with workers living under the 'credible threat' of job loss if their remuneration climbs too high to compete with robots and overseas workers.[26]

The problem with this story is that not all jobs can be exported abroad. Nor are all jobs technologically substitutable. At other historical junctures rapid technological change did not lead to a depression of wages.

An alternative explanation is that there's been a profound shift in the balance of power – from employees to employers, from workers to owners, from labour to capital – and one key reason for this is intense market concentration. The dominance of 'superstar firms' – the loss of competition in a particular market – has translated into the diminution of wages, particularly for the low-paid, both in the US and the UK.[27]

Consider how things should work in a genuinely free market. Different companies compete with one another for workers. Businesses bid up the wage to recruit workers from their rivals. In this Economics 101 world, there is a close connection between a worker's wages and their productivity. The company makes money, certainly. But I get paid properly in relation to what the company makes.[28] And in this world, if my company lowers pay, or doesn't adjust it for inflation, or pays me too little when offering new people jobs, it won't be able to hold onto me.

In a concentrated market, however, because there are fewer other companies to compete with my employer for my labour, my employer can pay me less. A business will offer me a lower wage and I'll take it because there's nowhere else I can go. I have no other options. There's not going to be a mass exodus of workers when a pay cut is announced.

In her book *The Economics of Imperfect Competition* (1933) the economist Joan Robinson coined the term 'monopsony' to describe this scenario – the labour market equivalent of monopoly.* In a situation where workers have limited options of who to work for, their wages will be set below the value of their contribution

---

* If a *monopoly* exists where a business is the sole *seller* of a good; a *monopsony* situation exists when a company is the sole *buyer* of a good. The classic example of a monopsony is a company coal town where there is one firm. Say you have been working in the pit your whole life with a good income until suddenly a new owner comes in and cuts wages by 10 per cent. You are working just as hard and productively as before. But now you get less money. Why? Because the firm has taken advantage of the fact that it knows you probably won't move. Its monopsony power enables it to set wages below the productivity of the workers in order to capture greater profits.

to output. What this allowed Robinson to say was that, in many cases, trade unions, far from inhibiting the free market, allowed for the restoration of just wages: that is, remuneration closer to what would be a competitive outcome.

Despite this danger, wages aren't usually considered an anti-trust issue. When regulators convene to contest market power, it is monopoly and not monopsony that they have in their sights. When they decide whether to allow a merger, or whether a certain company should be broken up, they are preoccupied with consumer prices alone. The effect on wages is not their concern. It is illegal for firms to merge for the purpose of dominating a labour market, certainly. But the sheer fact of industrial concentration, by itself, whatever the intention, has not proved sufficient for government action.

'Monopsony' is not just an indirect consequence of concentrated markets, however. Increasingly apparent is the way companies have abused market power to depress wages in more direct ways.

'If you hire a single one of these people, that means war,' Steve Jobs told Google's Sergey Brin. In 2005 six Silicon Valley companies – Apple, Google, Intel, Adobe, Intuit and Pixar – colluded to try and keep down the wages of their workers. Sharing wage scales, they agreed not to recruit employees from one another. The cost of labour was not being determined by the invisible hand of the market. People weren't being remunerated on merit, for what they were worth, or how productive they were being.

This was in Silicon Valley, but exactly the same kind of collusion has been exposed in the low-wage sector.

The *New York Times* published a startling exposé of widespread practice in the fast-food industry.[29] Buried deep in fast-food franchise agreements are obscure clauses that prohibit nearby franchisees of some of the industry's biggest players from hiring workers away from one another. Because the no-hiring clauses are signed between employers – for example, between two neighbouring franchises of a pizza chain – *employees* remain in the dark. But when they try switching jobs to get a pay rise they soon find they have no luck.

More common than downright collusion, because legal, are non-compete clauses, which prevent employees leaving previous employers for competitors. Again, non-compete clauses have long been routine among senior executives, designed as they are to stop them working for a competitor or starting a business, and gaining competitive advantage by exploiting confidential information about their previous company's operations.[30] That justification becomes less plausible the lower down the job-income scale you move, though that's exactly what's happened.

Take the case of Timothy Gonzalez. Gonzalez started working as a labourer for a construction firm at the age of 18. He was already a father. High school was the extent of his education. He was desperate for a job, and there weren't many options in front of him. The job he did get was 'pretty much shovelling dirt'. It paid a little over $10 an hour yet still included a non-compete clause enforceable within 350 miles of the company's home in Mississippi. 'All I heard – at that age and the situation I was in – was just, "If you want a pay cheque, sign here," and so I signed there and went to work.' However, four years later, when a better-paying job came up with a competitor, Gonzalez was sued for violating his non-compete agreement.[31]

The economist Alan Krueger has described non-compete clauses as part of a rigged labour market where employers act to prevent the forces of competition.[32] And again, by suppressing the forces of competition, wages are artificially depressed: first, because workers can't move to a higher-paying job; and second, because if they are unable to seek a higher-paying job elsewhere, they are unlikely to be able to bargain for a rise.[33]

The fate of families, then – the plight of the working poor – comes down, to a significant degree, to lack of competition. This means that resistance to corrective intervention in the labour market ensures and legitimates the perpetuation of in-work poverty. Thus, to the extent that the Right is committed to laissez-faire, to the extent that it has endorsed the evisceration of unions and resisted anti-trust enforcement, the Right has ignored its family values.

CORPORATE SOCIAL RESPONSIBILITY

The current configuration of the market serves to extract value from the poorest workers, and to the extent that the Right endorses that system, by insisting that the government leaves alone even anti-competitive markets, it undermines its avowed commitment to working families.

My argument so far has focused on *structure* – the way the market functions. But there is also the issue of *culture*. For it is not just the system that accounts for the stagnation of wages and pressure on the poorest families. We must also speak of the shift of norms, changing patterns in the behaviour, ideals and expectations of business elites. The economist Robert Solow dismissed the discussion of corporate culture as 'a blaze of amateur sociology'. Let's try our hand at that.

We are familiar with the statistics. Forty years ago, the CEO was making 20 times that of his (yes, his) average worker. Today it's a ratio of 300:1. We are familiar with the stories. The janitor once taken care of by his company, sharing some of its gains, but is shackled to his pay bracket regardless of his employer's profits. And we are familiar with the mantras. 'We aim to maximize shareholder value.'

Many have traced the evolution of this paradigm shift to round about 13 September 1970. 'The social responsibility of business', Milton Friedman pronounced in the *New York Times*, 'is to make profits.' The view caught on in major companies and business schools alike. Out with the 'mutuality of obligation' – dismissed as old-fashioned *noblesse oblige*; in with the imperative to make money for owners alone.[34]

The ideological underpinning of this abrogation of responsibility – this transformed conception of the firm – can be traced back to that staple abstraction of economic thought, *homo economicus*. In his famous 'invisible hand' passage in *The Wealth of Nations* Adam Smith writes:

[Each businessman] intends only his own gain, and he is in this, as in many other cases led by an invisible hand to promote an end that was no part of his intention ... By pursuing his own interest, he frequently promotes that of the society more effectually than when he really intends to promote it. I have never known much good done by those who affected to trade for the public good.[35]

Thus was born a normative ideal: the dollar-hunter, the rational decision-maker who acts in his best interests according to the information available to him, the economic actor capable of judging the comparative efficacy of means for obtaining wealth; always seeking the greatest amounts of goods with the smallest amount of labour.

Notice that the behaviour of the businessman isn't justified by saying something like 'Everyone has their own family to look after, so to be self-interested is understandable'. The profit motive isn't being presented as some kind of compromise, a necessary evil for the sake of survival. Not at all. Looking out for yourself is actually going to turn out to be the best way to look out for the other guy. And if you depart from the model, if you do try to '[affect] to trade for the public good'? Well, then you won't actually achieve your desired aim. So, on this account, the best way to be good is to be bad.[36]

What this picture of the coincidence of individual and collective welfare lends to firms is the ability to present conscious decisions as forms of necessity. If a management's relentless pursuit of profit via maximizing shareholder returns really will, in another of Smith's phrases, 'redound to the public interest', then the immediate costs on people can be justified as inevitable.

Take the 'fissuring' of the workplace since the 1980s – the way firms have shed their role as direct employers of the people working under their brand, by shunting out jobs deemed peripheral to their 'core competencies'. Delivery drivers who wear the uniforms of their lead businesses, but who in fact work for small, independent contractors; room cleaners employed not actually by the hotel where they spend their days – their *place* – but by a separate management company; chocolate packers receiving their pay cheque from a labour supplier and not the company whose name is on the bar: despite remaining invisible to consumers, employment has been drastically fragmented. Now companies can have it both ways: closely enforcing standards, dictating every last detail from the presentation of a burger to the order of cleaning tasks, while at the same time avoiding having to pay benefits and escaping liability for workplace injuries.[37]

For many, this transformation of the workplace flowed inevitably from the digital advances that have enabled work to be designed, monitored and managed by parties outside the corporation. What this technological determinism masks is the fact that it was a change in investment culture that dictated the technology be put to this particular use.

No less determined is the casualization of labour we are witnessing today. In the UK, zero-hours contracts – concentrated in low-wage jobs such as retail, hospitality and social care – have quadrupled over the last decade.[38] We have seen the impact of precarious employment on families. With no guaranteed minimum number of hours, workers have no idea what their income's going to be. The fluctuation in funds over the course of a month renders budgeting and planning ahead almost impossible. With no sickness pay, crisis management becomes very difficult. With no maternity and paternity pay, having children is difficult. With short notice of additional hours, raising those children is a nightmare.

Daniel Arthur provides a representative example. A delivery driver from Sheffield on a zero-hours contract, Daniel is reliant on his firm for his vehicle; his firm dictates the hours he can work, yet he is deemed to be self-employed. Although he was promised three shifts of eleven hours a night for a minimum of five nights a week, the work he has been given comes nowhere close. But, and here's the rub, he's paid not per shift but per delivery. He's told to sit in his van to wait until assignments come in and, when they don't, he's not paid. Once he was given the wrong address for a parcel delivery. The firm called him the next day and said he wouldn't get paid unless he delivered to the new address. Panicking, for a few hours he left his kids unsupervised. With an estimated pre-tax annual income of only £10,000, clearly that work had put great pressure on his marriage.[39]

There was nothing inevitable about this fundamental restructuring of work. Some people in the world chose to shift risk onto other people in the world. Zero-hours contracts serve as an effective management tool for a firm to adjust to fluctuations in demand. Under the guise of 'flexibility', largely chimerical given that the vast majority of those on zero-hours contracts want more hours, companies can simply adjust staffing levels during a downturn and avoid wage bills.

THE GREAT DISEMBEDDING

In his great text *The Great Transformation*, Karl Polanyi spoke of the market's ability to inflict 'lethal injuries to the institutions in which social existence is embedded'.[40] The family is one of those institutions – the site of our belonging; where we are embedded; where we are to learn how to work hard and live well; where virtue is inculcated, and love experienced as sheer gratuity. But today it is threatened not just by the erosion of traditional cultural norms but also by economic factors, and economic factors within our control – by both market manipulation and business culture. A commitment to family values means tackling the former and transforming the latter.

3

Sufficiency: Why the Left and Sexual Liberation Make Bad Bedfellows

They met at the after-party of a Hollywood awards ceremony. He was a star, she was tipsy, they were flirting. They had both been taking photographs. They compared cameras. They danced. 'It was like, one of those things where you're aware of the other person all night,' she said. 'We would catch eyes every now and then.' Before the night was over, he took her number. Before tomorrow had ended, he sent her a message. Before the week had ended, the date was on.[1]

An oyster bar on a boat on the Hudson. A warm September evening. The conversation was fine, but he, according to her, was keen to leave. 'He got the check and then it was, bada-boom, bada-bing, we're out of here.'

Back at his Manhattan apartment he promptly sat her on the kitchen counter and began to kiss her. 'In a second, his hand was on my breast.' Things escalated. He was undressing her, then himself. When he informed her he would get a condom, she responded, 'Whoa, let's relax for a sec, let's chill.' He settled for oral sex. First on her. Then on him. 'It was really quick. Everything was pretty much touched and done within ten minutes of hooking up, except for actual sex.'

Not that he didn't try that. But when he did, she told him, 'I didn't want to be engaged in that with him.' He backed off, momentarily, pouring more wine as she went to the bathroom. When she returned, he asked if she was all right. She answered that she didn't want to feel forced 'because then I'll hate you, and I'd rather not hate you'. 'Of course,' he replied, 'it's only fun if we're both having fun.'

Seconds later, however, he kissed her again and, to sanitize her account somewhat, made it clear he desired intercourse. This time she stood up. 'I really don't think I'm going to do this.' He backed down again, echoing her desire to 'chill', assuring her this time it would be with their clothes on. That made little difference. Soon he was trying to undress her again, until finally she said, 'You guys are all the fucking same', and told him she wanted to call a cab. Which, finally relenting, he did. She remembers the cab home: 'I cried the whole ride ... At that point I felt violated. That last hour was so out of my hands.'

The facts have been debated. The discussion has been endless. For many, the significance of the case is that it evinces a gross abuse of power. The man got what he wanted merely by virtue of being who he was – a star. He leveraged his fame to secure what he could not otherwise have got, which would have eluded him as a mere everyman. Even though the relationship was not strictly consummated, he overrode her wishes.

Others have questioned the veracity of the account, appalled at the assassination of the man's character based on one woman's anonymous testimony. The allegations were vindictive. She wanted something she didn't get, one commentator surmises – to be a star's girlfriend – and when she didn't get that, she gave a magazine 3,000 words of 'revenge porn'. That commentator continues: 'We're at warp speed now and the revolution – in many ways so good and so important – is starting to sweep up all sorts of people into its conflagration: the monstrous, the cruel, and the simply unlucky.'

For yet others, the fact is that he did not have sexual relations with that woman. Even if she is telling the truth, the woman may have felt uncomfortable, but the sexual relations they did have were consensual. And when she did object, to intercourse itself, he called a cab.

The question not being asked is whether the woman (assuming she was telling the truth) expected too much of the man that night. Was that unfair of her? To entertain a belief that flirting at the wedding might constitute some kind of wooing, might be an expression of genuine interest in her. That the romance on the Hudson might not prove a front. A quick fuck might turn out to be the beginning of a beautiful friendship, but she seemed to fear it might reduce the likelihood of that possibility. Was that wrong? Was it naïve to hold out hope that you guys are *not* all the fucking same?

———

Sexual liberation is often held up as one of the signal achievements of the countercultural Left, having given permission and encouragement to men and women alike to pursue their libidinal desires without fear of 'bourgeois' inhibitions, strictures or pieties. Alternatively, this liberation is cited by social conservatives of the Right as one of the more destructive psychological and social legacies of the selfish and self-absorbed Left. They have, so reasons the Right, weakened conventions essential to mutually respectful human relations, including those that once informed dating, courtship and marriage. Here I intend to step back from the opposing interpretations and explore the relation between the Left's historic critique of consumerism and its posture towards a largely norm-free sexual culture. Put in terms of this book, what happens to the principle of *sufficiency*, understood as satisfaction with material goods, when it comes to our carnal desires? Is there a compelling ideal or important value being expressed in one position – the left-wing package deal – but ignored in another? And if there is, would that matter? Why should we care if, owing to the contingent political factors, one view has been tacked onto another?

GETTING AND SPENDING

Consumere – to take up completely, devour, waste, spend.

It was this old pejorative connotation of the Latin word that a new generation of left-wing cultural critics appropriated in their interrogations of consumerism. Texts such as *The Critique of Everyday Life*, by Henri Lefebvre, Guy Debord's *Society of the Spectacle* and Jean Baudrillard's *The Consumer Society* assailed the rampant materialism of the society that emerged after the Second World War.

Capitalism had instilled, for Baudrillard, 'a compulsion to need and a compulsion to consume'. For Debord, in the West it was now the case that 'being is having' and 'human fulfilment is no longer equated with what one is but with what one possesses'. For Lefebvre 'the cult of the transitory' was 'the essence of [capitalist] modernity', rendering material objects things 'to be longed for, desired, then superseded and discarded'.

Take this insight of Lefebvre's first. Pre-modern peoples such as the Ming were collectors, certainly, but of old things. They treasured objects for their antiquity. But in capitalist modernity, out with the old, in with the new. In the seventeenth and eighteenth centuries north-western Europe experienced an avalanche of new products. In 1785 Adam Smith observed that people were filling their pockets with 'little conveniences' – from tweezer cases to decorative snuff boxes – and then purchasing coats with pockets for more stuff.[2]

The cult of the transitory suggests that consumerism has more to do with detachment than attachment. 'Attachment' suggests clinging to the things that have been bought, constantly returning to them, continuing to derive enjoyment from them. Attachment holds out the possibility of satisfaction. 'Detachment', by contrast, suggests the swift exhaustion of purchases as consumers become restless, and are then driven forward to buying new goods.[3]

What explains the cult of the transitory? What accounts for how quickly we move through our products and exhaust our stuff?

The new critics of consumerism were fixated on the question of the formation of desire. They were riveted by the relation, in a complex society, between the accumulation of goods and the stimulation of basic human appetites – first, our desire to live a vicarious existence; second, our obsession with social status.

Take these in turn. The first thing we want is to be *multiple*. The life we have may not be especially impoverished. It may not in itself be sorely lacking. It is just singular. And we want to know what it is like to be other people. We want to try out a variety of existences, dress ourselves in borrowed robes.[4]

Advertising simultaneously answers to and amplifies this, responds to and reinforces it, promising us in goods and in experiences a vicarious existence. For example, an advertisement from a high-end American department store, Neimus Marcus, parades before us a poised Parisian lady. She wears an elegant *chapeau* and *haute couture* coat. The advert reads:

ATTITUDE IS disposition with regard to people or things.
ATTITUDE IS wearing the correct thing at the correct time.
ATTITUDE IS a seam.
ATTITUDE IS exactly sized.
ATTITUDE IS a mode.
ATTITUDE IS an evaluation.
ATTITUDE IS strolling the avenue.
ATTITUDE IS Neiman Marcus.[5]

She is someone we will never be, but to whom purchases might permit us to pretend.

The phenomenon of celebrity is almost too obvious to mention. Products become substitutes for lives we will never lead. While we wait for our band to make it, or to be given the right role, we live vicariously through getting and spending. What makes this syndrome peculiar to our era is the way that global capitalism has brought so many different ways of life closer to us than ever before. We can see vividly a greater number of people who we want to be.

The combined fact of the futility of this project for the self and the interminable number of lives on offer accounts for the insatiability of the consumer appetite. Our unwillingness to countenance the fact we only have one life to live drives us to the ceaseless accumulation of material goods.

Secondly, commodities are markers of social status, bought and sold not for their 'use value', their functionality or even beauty, but for their 'sign value', their capacity for differentiation.

'Conspicuous consumption' had been named at the turn of the nineteenth century by Thorstein Veblen to describe the ostentatious expenditure patterns of the elite. He described the dynamic according to which the leisure class sought to distinguish itself by means of consumption. Since a wealthy minority had what it needed, consumption was able to become fundamentally competitive, he observed. And because status is inherently a zero-sum game, since for one person to win another must lose, the production of prestige goods is wasteful. The investment of time and energy does not secure improvements in 'human well-being on the whole'.

What Baudrillard did was to take Veblen and extend his theory to everyone. In an era of greater affluence, the whole of society could be organized around the display of commodities through which individuals gain prestige. This second desire, for status, also involves a dialectical relation with The System – an interplay of our basic instincts and the institutions that play upon them to create new needs for new products.

What was wrong with any of this? Where were the grounds for objections? For the new generation of critics, it signalled clear evidence of deep alienation. Modern man had become estranged from his true needs and true nature.

It's easy to discard this as patrician disdain, or as trading on the assignation of false consciousness – thinking that people (in this case consumers) are acting against their own interests, even though they take themselves to be doing what they want to do. Which might be true, if the Left's starting-point wasn't the incontestable paradox that humankind's final achievement of material abundance had not secured universal happiness. In other words, mankind's malaise had to be reflective of *something*, even if people could not articulate what it was.

It was not just the fate of the individual consumer – that is, what he was doing to himself – that was the source of consternation. The critics were concerned with the ramifications of the creation of a culture, if by 'culture' we mean the establishment of a distinct way of organizing experience which communicates ideals and embeds norms, a transmittable body of beliefs and practices, rituals and roles. What was the impact of a materialistic culture on those who had no part in it but still found themselves subject to it? Those who knew no other world?

ORDERING A PERSON

In her reportage piece for *Vanity Fair* on the phenomenon of the 'dating' app Tinder, Nancy Jo Sales interviewed three investment bankers in their twenties.[6] As they drink their beers and swipe their glowing screens, she enquires whether they are organizing dates. Not just one, but two or even three, they tell her. 'You can't be stuck in one lane ... There's always something better,' says Alex. 'If you had a reservation somewhere and then a table at [another restaurant] opened up, you'd want to go there.' He continues:

Guys view everything as a competition. Who's slept with the best, hottest girls? You could talk to two or three girls at a bar and pick the best one, or you can swipe a couple hundred people a day – the sample size is so much larger. It's setting up two or three Tinder dates a week and, chances are, sleeping with all of them, so you could rack up 100 girls you've slept with in a year.

Sales discovers that Alex has slept with five 'Tinderellas' in eight days, a feat his room-mates readily vouch for, and envy too. His text game is second to none – that is, his ability to bed someone on the basis of a few texts while, crucially, ensuring they know he's not interested in a relationship.

Alex is a consumer extraordinaire, flicking through catalogues at frenetic speed, on the hunt for a bargain, obsessed with increasing optionality, the shopping even more exhilarating than the purchase.

If choice is the attraction of Tinder for Alex, the key for fitness instructor Nick is price. 'I hooked up with three girls, thanks to the Internet off of Tinder, in the course of four nights, and I spent a total of $80 on all three girls.' He ostensibly goes over to their place to

77

smoke weed and watch a movie. After 15 minutes of talking he hooks up. 'Afterwards she goes, "Oh my God, I wasn't gonna have sex with you." And I was like, "Well you did a pretty shit job of that one."'

Dan, meanwhile, another investment banker, values the ease of the exchange. 'It's like ordering Seamless [an online food-delivery service]. But you're ordering a person.'

Are Alex, Nick and Dan outliers? Or are they representative Tinder users? Whatever the case, the technology itself, used by over a hundred million people, inscribes the attitudes they unabashedly express. This technology fundamentally recasts what you need to know about someone, a few words of self-representation and a face, when you seek to be intimate with them.

Meanwhile, on campus, 'I'm basically in a paradise of girls I'm attracted to. Everyone is fucking each other,' says one freshman. According to the most recent sociological studies, what is new about this culture is the strong expectation that hooking up is what one should be doing. And in such a culture, how can the self-reported female preoccupation with 'fuckability' be interpreted as anything other than the penetration of the objectifying male gaze?

You don't have to look long at our sexual culture to feel the resonance of the Left's critique of consumerism. Is not the erotic market-place characterized by the cult of the transitory, in which people too are treated as 'something to be longed for, desired, then superseded and discarded'? Does not the experience of uninhibited choice in the economic sphere impress itself upon our comportment in the sexual? Are we not often compelled to upgrade to a better deal, finding brand loyalty increasingly difficult?

Here too we confront the complexity of the formation of desire – the dialectical relation between the expression and manipulation of needs.

Take firstly, the way pornography works, and its similarity to advertising. At the age of eight Drew discovered *Girls Gone Wild* on a TV channel at home. Next, he discovered HBO's late-night soft-core pornography. At 14 he discovered sites on his phone. The videos both satiated existing desires and also stimulated new ones – specifically, future positions with future girlfriends. By 15 he had become concerned that porn was having an effect on the way he looked at girls at school – the size of their breasts, the intensity of their responses, their willingness to oblige in the acts the stars so willingly performed for the men on the shows. The world of spectacle was starting to 'act back' on his real life.

Pornography, just like advertising, plays on our desire to be multiple. The plethora of people and the variety of situations paraded by porn allows for vicarious existence, all manner of situations, exotic encounters shorn of all context. And this in turn means that when real sex is to be had, it is shaped by the deep desire for diversity. What will the body to this face look like? How will I experience its difference? In what ways will it be new?

Secondly, sexual consumption too is conspicuous and competitive. 'Guys view everything as a competition,' we heard Alex say above. While at school and college sex may (mostly) happen in private, partners are secured in public. The rituals of initiation are overt. The logic is not that of the private affair. It is of display. And if in the eating clubs, fraternities and societies that comprise the community, belonging – finding a place in a giddy world – is of critical importance, and sexual conquests are the currency, then the culture of emulative sexual consumption is perpetuated ad infinitum. To belong is to compete.

What is the effect of sexual consumerism? We saw how the pervasive dissatisfaction in a society of material abundance provoked critics to insist on a theory of alienation. Well, what are we to make of the news coming in from college?

In her sociological study *American Hookup*, Lisa Wade tells the story of Owen, raised in a small farming town in central California. An environment where everyone knew one another intimately made sexual experimentation rare and secretive. College therefore came as a whole new world – 'an endless supply of potential partners and more anonymity than he'd ever dreamed of'. In his freshman year Owen sought out sexual encounters with 'gusto'. And success. By his second year, though, he had started to feel uncomfortable. 'I find it especially hard to try to smooth out a relationship with a girl whom I barely know beyond what colour underwear she wears.' He admits his anxiety – 'When I think about my sex life, it feels like my insides tie themselves tight together' – and its toll – 'Worrying about it saps a lot of time and energy.' By the end of the year he had sworn off sexual encounters. 'I can't handle another negative sexual relationship in my life. My heart might break.' Wade concludes from her wider research:

There is nothing unique about [Owen's] disappointment ... There is a persistent malaise: a deep,
indefinable disappointment. Students find that their
sexual experiences are distressing or boring ... They
are frustrated and feel regret, but they're not sure
why.[7]

THE SEXUAL REVELATION

If the critique of consumerism is so applicable to our
sexual culture, why is the cultural Left reluctant to
act on it? Why has it been so reticent to denounce our
sexualized culture as vociferously as it has, so vitally, our
sexist one? The answer, I propose, is because within the
left-wing package deal is an unwavering commitment to
sexual liberation.

The sexual revolution was based on a sexual
revelation. By 'revelation' I mean the emergence of a
new set of beliefs which cannot be wholly reduced to
material factors. The sexual revolution was not just an
explosion of erotic activity as a result of, say, changed
material conditions – most obviously, the technological
development of the pill. The sexual revolution was a
signal instance of a paradigm shift, a transformation
of human consciousness, the generation of a new
'plausibility structure'.

The sexual revelation was that the fundamental
cause of our ailment is repression. Human potential
was thwarted by traditional *mores*, and only the
overthrow of renunciatory controls – the disciplines
that hedged in desire – would lead to the flourishing
of individuals and secure the peace of society. As the
guru of sexual liberation, Freud's student Wilhelm

Reich, put it, the 'armouring' of the individual against instinct 'results inevitably in a limitation of the total ability to live' and is 'the chief reason for the loneliness of so many people in the midst of collective living'.[8] More was at stake than increasing the frequency of orgasms. Freedom from anti-sexual taboos is not just about instant gratification but about breaking down the 'wall between sex and life'.

In March 1967 the young British playwright Joe Orton told his lover Kenneth Halliwell that sex was 'the only way to smash up the wretched civilization'. He elaborated in his diary: 'Yes. Sex is the only way to infuriate them. Much more fucking and they'll be screaming hysterics in next to no time.'[9] Meanwhile his literary counterpart in the US, Norman Mailer, wrote of the sex life of the nation in the decade prior to the 1960s: 'these have been years of conformity and depression. A stench of fear has come out of every pore in American life, and we suffer from a collective failure of nerve.'[10]

The wretched civilization that needed to be defied was one that afforded priority to abstinence, whether embodied in the celibate life or in a chaste youth, which had to be overhauled. For centuries, the thought went, the church had maintained men and women in a state of unrelieved guilt by refusing to sanction the relief of the psychic tension between Libido and Ego. Ascetical practices, theological injunctions that desire should be 're-channelled' – whether through universalizing Eros outwards to all men or referring it upwards to God – now fell under suspicion as but camouflage for fear of the natural and uncontrollable.

The Christian sexual ethic was cast aside as anti-life, anti-corporeal, emasculating. Historians have debunked the self-understanding of these '60s radicals by pointing to evidence of the prevalence of promiscuity prior to the Second World War. In Britain in the 1910s and 1920s illegitimacy, prostitution and venereal disease were extremely common, while contraceptives had been used long before the 1960s, with effective diaphragms available from 1918 and contraceptive jelly from 1932. 'Many people', one historian concludes, 'were simply unable to keep to their high standards.'

But that's exactly the point. There *were* standards – attested to by the expectation of, say, a shotgun wedding – and it was their subversion that was at issue.

This gnawing at norms led to consent being enshrined as the sole constraint on sex. What separated morally problematic from morally unproblematic sexual practice was solely the freedom under which, in a particular moment, it was secured. As a result, law rather than custom comes to the fore as the chief regulator of the courses of human action, sharply differentiating between the absolutely fine and the quite unforgivable. The triumph of sex-positive feminism since the 1980s attests to just how unwavering liberalism's commitment to the sexual revolution has proven. In her seminal essay 'Lust Horizons', Ellen Willis pushed back against feminists who thought to challenge the legacy of the sexual revolution on grounds that it resulted in the unleashing of male desire. Women, Willis thought, had not been sexually emancipated only to have their freedom curbed by interrogations of the nature of desire and the suspicion that 'our most passionate convictions about sex do not necessarily reflect our real desires [but] are as likely to be aimed at repressing the pain of desires we long ago decided were too dangerous to acknowledge, even to ourselves'.[11] The result of that suspicion was to curb not only men's but also women's freedom by reintroducing neo-Victorian authoritarianism – marriage as the safest context for non-oppressive sex. But what if we took women at their word, Ellis asks, and believed that 'women really want free love', albeit 'on equal terms that do not now exist'?

PAYING ATTENTION

So the Left's enduring commitment to the sexual revolution is what explains why it has not applied its powerful critique of consumerism to our sexual culture. More needs to be said, though, about why that inconsistency is a problem. The point is not to sit back smugly, with cold evaluative satisfaction, and expose internal contradictions. We must ask: which aspect of the good is being obscured by this bundling of positions? Differently put, what mistake about value has been admitted by way of this conjoining of views on the Left? Which positive value is it exactly that is being expressed in one part of the left-wing package deal – the critique of consumerism – but ignored in another part – its commitment to the sexual revolution? What does the Left get right about what is wrong with consumerism? And, therefore, what is the problem about the sexual revolution?

At the heart of consumerism is the cult of the transitory – exhausting what we have in a continual lust for what we don't (yet) have. The power of the critique, in my view, is to expose why this dynamic first and foremost constituted an *aesthetic* mistake.

Aestheticism can be defined as 'viewing every object as you would a work of art'.[12] What does it take to view a work of art? Viewing a work of art requires sustained attention. It requires being immersed in it, completely absorbed by it. A striking painting may 'hail us', certainly; we may talk of being 'blown away' by it. But when we say it 'cries out for our attention', we mean it demands we examine it further, undistractedly, with pure focus – taking in the colour and the composition, the form and the figures. That's how we will wring out its meaning, get the most out of it, by coming back to it again and again, precisely by not letting it wash over us. It requires us to be in active mode.

'For anything to become interesting,' Flaubert wrote, 'you simply have to look at it for a long time.' Reflecting on Flaubert's philosophy of aestheticism, the brilliant American essayist Mark Greif writes:

> The discipline is to learn to see the rest of the world in just that same way. Art becomes a training for life ... Over time, and with practice, the work of art will become less effective at stimulating these art experiences than your renewed encounters with the world will be ... '*Look more closely*' is the basic answer of the aesthete to any failure of experience.[13]

Note that concentrating on what is in front of us is a discipline, and not just one for those of us predisposed to discipline, naturally good at concentration. Cultivating the habit of attention is a universal challenge and a universal possibility.

Notice too how counterintuitive the practice is. Aestheticism is not a Romantic philosophy of ecstasy and instant gratification; it involves placing things in history. 'You simply have to look at it for a long time.' Seeing, real seeing, is not immediate but takes time.

The problem with consumerism, and the source of our dissatisfaction, is that we do not stay long enough with our goods to appreciate them. In addition, crucially, to take time to appreciate our good entails limitation. There are only a limited number of items we can fully enjoy in the way described above, with which we can seek renewed encounters. This means that attending to things requires excluding others. Making the most of some opportunities means actively forgoing others. Paradoxically, the aesthetic orientation liberates us by constraining us, as we forsake the endless array of options before us and impose self-restraint on ourselves.

In his first major book, *Either/Or*, the nineteenth-century Danish philosopher Søren Kierkegaard wrote an imaginary letter from an older married man, Judge William, to an unnamed younger bachelor. The letter is called 'The Aesthetic Validity of Marriage'. The title is meant to sound paradoxical.

Over the course of his long epistle Judge William argues passionately that the highest poetic form is 'historical love', when one places the relationship in time – that is, when a couple agrees to be together indefinitely, moving forward into the future together.

Judge William begins by conceding that literature hardly glorifies historical love itself. The quest for the lady's hand, the toil and trouble knights and adventurers undertake for it – that is the stuff of our most cherished legends. But there those books end, with the achievement of marriage. What we never get, because undramatic by comparison, are accounts of the course of the marriage itself (unless it is troubled, of course). But what escapes literature is what affords the greatest aesthetic value. Why is this?

It has to do with the nature of repetition. With material objects, true appreciation, I propose, involves forgoing immediacy and committing to renewed contact with them. Similarly, with love, only repetition – the experience of the same person afforded by relationships that endure over time – yields a fuller appreciation of his or her beauty.

Kierkegaard employs a lovely metaphor for this. It's like gazing at a stream, he says. In one regard it is always the same: the same soft sound, the colour of the riverbed beneath the current, fishes that slide under the cover of the flowers. But in another way, it is 'rich in change'. Its appearance alters under different aspects. Blanched in moonlight, for example, it looks different. In the same way historical love is 'dear to one who knows it, dear to him because he knows it'.[14]

A constant return to the same partner might deliver delight, certainly. But Kierkegaard is hinting at something more than mere repetition. There is a greater delight which derives from love 'referring its experiences back to itself'. Historical love builds upon itself.

It doesn't start from scratch every time but works off old memories to create new experiences.[15]

There is nothing sentimental about this. As with the appreciation of goods, relationships become a discipline; something we work at. And one that again requires limitation. Radicalizing the thought above, true appreciation of one's partner forswears all others. Making the most of this opportunity means actively forgoing others.

NO HARM DONE?

'First and foremost, an aesthetic mistake ...' What I have tried to argue about sexual consumerism is that it is the cult of the transitory, and that the compulsion, bluntly, to 'move through' people as we 'move through things' entails the loss of vision. It is a failure of attention. Fleeting sexual experiences fail on aesthetic grounds because they lack the time it takes to appreciate a person fully. And if aesthetic experience is a constitutive part of a flourishing human life, then it could be said that fleeting sexual experiences prevent us making a success of life.

To speak of the aesthetic invalidity of sexual consumerism, to locate our critique on grounds of human flourishing, is to say something about why the consumer extraordinaire loses out on life. It is to concentrate on what it does to them – the person doing the consuming. But what about the other person, the one on the other side of the deal, the one on the receiving end of such sexual consumerism? The person objectified. The person consumed. Can we say they are harmed or wronged in some way by failing to be appreciated? To answer this, it is necessary to move from an aesthetic critique of sexual consumerism to an ethical one.

In proceeding to an ethical critique, we arrive, at last, at the question that may have been nagging you for a while. For the class of sexual experiences we've had in view are thoroughly consensual ones. Does it make sense to say I can harm someone who fully consents to sex?

Think first, but not too much, about a different class of sexual experiences: fully consensual sado-masochistic ones. Having agreed to try out this alternative form of sexual practice, a couple arrives at the decision of who will assume the submissive role and who the dominant. It so happens that the person who opts for the 'sub' has an unhealthy conception of themselves, having long viewed themselves as worthless. Old traumas are playing themselves out in new forms of sexual expression as they instinctively choose to be on the receiving end of pain and humiliation. How should we evaluate such a case?

We would probably want to say, first, that that person is hurting themselves – that what they are doing is bad for them. But what about what the 'dom' does in carrying out the 'sub's' freely formed request to be treated in this way? It seems to me that to treat someone in ways that re-inscribe their sense of inadequacy, to verify that person's compromised sense of self, is to wrong that person, regardless of consent. Participating in that is a terrible thing to do to someone. In receiving back from another an untrue, destructive conception of what you are and of the value you have, you have been harmed.

Now think back to the kind of ephemeral consensual encounters we've had in view. Think back to Alex, the Tinder addict. If sex is a speech-act, then what is he saying to the person he hooks up with for one night? Surely he is saying they are dispensable. He is saying to a person of irreplaceable value that they are replaceable, which means he is lying to them. He is offering back to them an untrue, destructive conception of what they are and the value they have. In pursuing pleasure independent of relationship, the sexual consumer is using the person and failing to provide what the philosopher Talbot Brewer terms 'an external validation of [the other person's] status as valuable in themselves rather than merely an instrument for bringing about states of affairs'.[16]

THE SEXUALIZATION OF CHILDHOOD

It is not just the specific harm to the individual that is at issue. As we saw in its searing critique of consumerism, it is also the creation of culture that concerns the Left, defined as 'the distinct way of organizing experience which communicates ideals and embeds norms, a transmittable body of beliefs and practices, rituals and roles'. What is the effect of a culture on those who had no part in it but still found themselves subject to it: children, for instance? Can we speak of 'harm' in this regard?

For the Left, children are victims of a materialistic culture. The Left is not slow to unleash invectives against marketing to children; it has been enduringly alert to the way in which the explosion in children's expenditure attests to the commodification of children as customers in their own right. The Left has charted how the quantification of children's buying power became big business; it has highlighted how, because of the influence of children's choices on parents' purchases, and their technological savvy, it has proved efficacious to advertise directly to children; and it has exposed how armies of researchers have been dispatched to watch children at play in order to understand what they would do in shops.[17] Marketers have become involved in shaping the desires of children and forming them as social beings – all to the end of producing customers for their client companies.

But the Left does not stop there. It may have failed to apply its critique of consumerism to our sexual culture at large, but it has most definitely decried the sexualization of childhood. Marketing has not only sought to mould little consumers but has also created 'sex children'.[18] Dolls dressed in miniskirts and fishnet stockings, clothing ranges including thong underwear for seven-to-ten-year-olds (and slogans like 'wink wink'), fashion shows where adult models appear as children but in lingerie – profits accrue to the corporations that can most effectively cause a child to objectify herself.

But that is as far as the critique goes. It stops there. It pulls up lame. The critique remains stunted because the Left's commitment to the sexual revolution prevents it from acknowledging the forms of *consensual* sexual activity that serve powerfully to objectify children.

Take the free pass given to Brook Sexual Health, a charity focusing on 'sexual health and wellbeing for under-25s', which has developed a 'Traffic Light Tool' to evaluate different types of sexual-related activity. The charity shows no hesitation in giving the green light to 13-year-olds to 'consenting oral and/or penetrative sex with others of the same or opposite gender who are of similar age and developmental ability', thus licensing young people to break the law.[19] But the really revealing aspect of the exercise is what does *not* warrant a red light. 'Outside of safe and healthy behaviour' is included, of course, non-consensual sex. But no mention is made of disembedded sexual activity – of hooking up, of ephemeral encounters. Mention is made of degradation, humiliation, exploitation, but there is no suggestion that any of this could occur within the context of consensual sex.

Nor is it just that fleeting sexual encounters are being tolerated. The commitment to sexual liberation has led to them being actively encouraged.

As a teenager, I wanted to spend the weekends at the houses of friends whose parents endorsed 'learning from experience'. This was because 'learning from experience' gave *carte blanche* for hooking up (not something, I should add, at which I was very successful). The recommendation of what the godfather of liberalism, John Stuart Mill, termed 'experiments in living' doesn't simply constitute a giving of permission for being sexually active: that is, it's not a kind of indulgence. It was the active promotion of it as a form of self-discovery.*

But what kind of relation to the other does this form of self-discovery require? If the aim is 'perceiving practically the worth of different modes of life', it seems

---

* Mill, in 'On Liberty' (1859) recommends what he calls 'experiments in living' as the necessary step towards achieving individuality. How do you become an individual? You have to try things out. Rather than taking our cue from custom, bowing before received tradition, or succumbing to authority, it is through experimentation, the sheer accumulation of experience, that we come to 'perceive practically the worth of different modes of life'.

that a plurality of relationships is required. Otherwise comparison would be impossible. Which means each relationship has to be deemed ahead of time as ephemeral. A single relationship will not suffice. Instead, relationships required for self-discovery are ones that must expire. And when the relationship is an encounter, more properly, the individual needs the other to fulfil his own individuality. Love would in fact impede the self-realization, and therefore by definition the other becomes a mere means to my end, a mere object of use.

I recently became a father to a daughter. Maybe I'm being over-protective, but I want her to get to a nunnery, and quickly. The alternative, a sexual health class, is unbearable. For to teach sex as being healthy or unhealthy implies everyone should be having sex, just as a class on 'healthy versus unhealthy eating' pictures consuming food as some kind of norm. Starving yourself of sex becomes as unnatural as starving yourself of food.[20] Abstinence becomes an eating disorder.

I don't want her to be hurt: that's the long and short of it. I don't want the absolute gift to male adolescents that is the imperative to 'learn from experience' to eventuate in my daughter's objectification. I don't want her to grow up in a world in which she is commodified under the cover of consent.

THE INSUFFICIENCY OF CONSENT

We began this chapter with the devastation of that celebrity's date that fateful evening in his Manhattan apartment. The point of the story was to illustrate the relation between two tragedies. The first was the abuse of power evinced by a celebrity's sexual advances. The second was its significance as a paradigm case of sexual consumerism. 'You guys are all the fucking same ...'

We must conclude by situating what we have said in the extraordinary moment in which we find ourselves. Thus far, one of the signal achievements of #MeToo has been to put pressure on the notion of consent by expanding the category of assault to include women, and sometimes men, subjected to people 'skilled in the abusive leveraging of their outsized power'.[21] First to fall, of course, have been prominent people in positions of power. But following soon after have been those who abuse power on a more familiar scale. As Alexandra Schwartz of *The New Yorker* names them, the 'friends, lovers, acquaintances, teachers, colleagues, bosses, the countless anonymous strangers who have forced their way forever into their targets' memories with indelible words and deeds that they, no doubt, have long forgotten'.[22]

One outworking of power here is that those predators have remained confident they are in a position to get away with it; those who forced themselves upon their victims safe in the knowledge that they could point back and, with impunity, conflate silence with consent.

The upshot of my argument in this chapter is that, just as notional consent can prove no bulwark against sexual harassment – that is, sexual harassment can take place in notionally consensual relations – so notional consent is no bulwark against commodification and the moral failure to recognize a person.*

A MATTER OF FLOURISHING

Behind every moral critique lies a picture of flourishing, a picture of what it means to make a success of life (another definition of the Greek word for happiness, *eudaimonia*). Attacks presuppose defences, and the ideal being defended in the Left's compelling critique of consumerism is that of a life satisfied with what it has, a life no longer defined by its struggle for yet more of the goods it has already accrued. My aim in this chapter has been to view our sexual culture in light of the principle of sufficiency and to find wanting this life of wanting. The consistent application of the principle would see us resting content with the relationships we have. And resting content is not passive: it requires radical commitment, binding oneself to the other, to *one* other.

---

* It is crucial to recognize the *distinction* as well as the relation between these two problems with consent. I mean in no way to acquiesce in the argument, emanating from some conservative quarters, that the source of our sexual harassment problem is our having given up on conservative sexual *mores*. The sexual harassment being exposed in our time is of a kind that has existed as long as there are power differentials and people (mostly, but not solely, men) who have been driven by sexualized needs to assert domination.

4

The Sanctity of Life: What's Pro-Life about an AR-15?

Ready, aim, fire, kill. A single shot was all it took. Every morning of his adult life Gail Gerlach, a 56-year-old plumber from Spokane, Washington, would strap on the holster of his 9mm handgun before going to work. But on 25 March 2013 he wouldn't just carry the gun: he would pull it out.

Brendon Kaluza-Graham was a 27-year-old convicted car thief. He must have thought this was an easy one. Gerlach had left his vehicle idling in his driveway – a 1997 Chevrolet Suburban jammed full with his tools and supplies. All Brendon had to do was jump in, slam the door and take off. The rush: the thrill of it all. As he drove off, he probably thought he'd got away with it until ... *crack* ... a bullet shot from at least 40 yards away pierced the rear window and struck him in the back of the head. He was killed instantly. He slumped over the wheel. The driverless vehicle lurched on two blocks before finally careering into a garage.

In court Gerlach pleaded self-defence to a manslaughter charge. Even though Kaluza-Graham had been driving away from the house, Gerlach claimed to have been 'in imminent danger of substantial bodily injury to himself'. The jury found Gerlach innocent, subsequently reimbursing him over $220,000 for legal bills and expert witnesses, yet not all were celebrating the outcome. 'He had hopes and dreams,' said Ann Kaluza, Brendon's grandmother, but 'was made into a poster boy for the angst of the community, a sacrificial lamb. That's not right.' Another friend of Brendon's family gave this interpretation: 'I'm worried that the community hears it's OK to shoot someone. His perceived threat was not reality. They said that was good enough to shoot someone.'

Gail Gerlach is not only an outspoken gun advocate but also a passionate anti-abortion activist. As an avowed Reaganite conservative, he cannot fathom how a society that prohibits prostitution, class-A drugs, even driving without a seatbelt, can tolerate the killing of an unborn child. He belongs to the lobbying group 'Pro Life Rocks'. In one internet post he gave passionate expression to his views: '[I]t is a human right to have life, and no one's right to take it away at any stage ... No one would be safe if we cannot protect the right to life.'[1]

———————

I thought I was prepared for it. Coming from a country where the party of the Right was pro-choice, I anticipated it would be strange to find there was even a debate about abortion. I had been told conservatives nurse a grievance, given it was the judiciary and not the legislature that legalized abortion and the decision was thereby perceived as undemocratic. (This has never been an issue in the UK since abortion was legalized by an Act of Parliament in 1967.) I had read too of the controversy surrounding government funding of abortions through Planned Parenthood – again alien to me, given that abortions had always been available on the NHS, our system of socialized medicine, for which I've always had a certain respect.

Then I landed. The multicoloured scrawl of the placards. 'A PERSON – NO MATTER HOW SMALL!' 'CHOOSE LIFE. YOUR MOM DID!' 'UNIQUE FROM DAY ONE!' The sheer amount of airtime. The prayer vigils. The marches. I had seen pictures of Martin Luther King addressing hundreds of thousands congregated between the Capitol and the Lincoln Memorial. I was astounded to see the anniversary of *Roe v. Wade*, the US Supreme Court's landmark decision to legalize abortion, could draw the same size crowd. Only then, I guess, did I realize how defining the issue is in American culture. (Even to term it an 'issue' is unacceptably bathetic.) I saw how abortion serves as a litmus test for candidates seeking office, as the strict condition for membership in a political community. You could not waver. You could not *not* know your mind. And there was no (longer) room for compromise. The days of 'safe, *rare* and legal' – the Clintonian compromise, which tried to affirm the conservative cause to reduce the number of abortions – were well and truly over. The abortion issue was a vortex sucking into itself questions of identity and poverty, race and patriarchy, questions about the limits of the state and the proper scope of public concern.

I also thought I was ready to face the firearms. At home we heard about the high-school massacres. We read profiles of the perpetrators. We gleaned something of the political deadlock. I knew there were lots of people who liked guns and didn't want to surrender them. Still, once more I wasn't really prepared. I didn't expect advertisements falling out of the supermarket coupons for a CM15 .223 Rem AR Semi-Auto Rifle with Red Dot Sight priced at $699.99 and 22/45 Lite Anodized .22 LR Semi-Auto Pistol from Ruger priced at $499.99. Nor was I prepared for how brazenly young men would walk into my local diner packing heat. Or the furore at my local gym over gun control. Forget about the debate about transgender bathrooms. Here the question was over access for armed men.

At the heart of the Republican package deal is the principle of the sanctity of life. Derived from the Latin for 'holy' (*sanctus*), the sanctity of life names a conviction about the inviolable status of every human being including, crucially, the newone, and thus underpins the Right's opposition to abortion. My aim in this chapter is to explore whether that value is expressed or ignored in another position found in the Republican package deal – the passionate opposition to gun control.

It might seem a bit rich for an Englishman to proffer a critical appraisal of American gun culture. For does not the insistence on the right to bear arms hark back to the historic reaction to the threat posed by British remote rule? Should this historical irony prove appropriate discouragement from venturing any further into this fraught area?

We have on several occasions now identified the contingency of the factors by which principles are distributed across the political spectrum. The formation of package deals owes its existence in large part to the political machinations of elites who have sought to foist all-encompassing ideologies upon us. Abortion is no different. Before coming to evaluate the sanctity of the life, it is worth appreciating how it came to be incorporated into the Republican package deal.

NIXON GOES TO ROME

Nixon wanted the Catholic vote. That's the long and short of it. The pro-life movement did not *begin* as a reaction to the legalization of abortion in 1973. The origins of pro-life activism in the twentieth century preceded *Roe v. Wade* by decades. That story is forgotten because the people who swelled the ranks of the campaigns are not those we expect to find. The men and women who mobilized to prevent liberalization were New Deal Democrats – Catholics who called for state social programmes, government aid to the poor and a living wage for workers. They had not bought into other political-economic views we now find within the Republican package deal and which were explored in Chapter 2. The pro-lifers were old-fashioned liberals committed to the principle of inclusivity that we explored in Chapter 1, convinced it was the responsibility of the government to care for the needy, the prerogative of the law to protect the vulnerable.

What's more, after the Second World War the pro-life cause was folded into the campaign for universal human rights, led by Democrats such as Eleanor Roosevelt and Catholic intellectuals such as Jacques Maritain. In 1947 the National Catholic Welfare Conference, the political and social justice organization of American Catholic bishops, presented the United Nations with a template for a human rights declaration which, alongside 'the right to education', the 'right to collective bargaining' and 'the right to assistance from society', recommended that the future declaration open with an unequivocal recognition of 'the right to life and bodily integrity *from the moment of conception*'.[2]

Few evangelical Protestants, by contrast, lobbied against liberalization. Neither influential magazines such as *Christianity Today* nor denominations such as the Southern Baptist Convention weighed in, perhaps for the very reason that Catholics did. All this was to change after *Roe v. Wade*.

During his first term as President, Nixon had pursued a decidedly pro-choice agenda, appointing abortion rights advocates to the administration who eased abortion restrictions, speaking to Congress on 'the problems of population growth' before signing into law a National Center for Family Services and mandating that all military bases grant requests for abortions even if that clashed with state and local laws.

All that changed when he came to see his chances of re-election hinged on bringing Catholics into the fold. He shamelessly reversed his position. Abortion was an issue he wanted to 'hit hard', he told his infamous aide H. R. Haldeman. 'The unborn have rights also', he was soon pronouncing publicly.

Aghast at the Supreme Court's decision in *Roe v. Wade* in 1973, and then dismayed by the Democrats' subsequent decision to make their peace with legalization (opposing the Human Rights Amendment which aimed to negate Roe by guaranteeing the rights of the newone in the Constitution, and then electing the pro-choice

Jimmy Carter), the Catholics were suddenly rich political pickings. Ronald Reagan, who had legalized abortion in California in 1967, seized the opportunity. In 1979 he sent a letter to a prominent pro-life congressman, Henry Hyde, which, as Reagan had hoped, was quickly leaked. 'The cause of life itself,' Hyde told his followers, 'had been handed a most significant opportunity to make a major advance on the national scene.' Next Reagan sent a senator to the historically non-partisan annual March for Life in Washington.

Victory for Reagan in 1980 did not, however, secure the outcomes the pro-life movement so desperately sought. None of the proposed versions of the Human Rights Amendment made it out of committee. Nevertheless, as the battleground shifted to nominations to the Supreme Court, pro-lifers, in the words of the historian Daniel K. Williams, 'felt that they had no choice but to link their movement's fortunes with those of the GOP.'[3]

THE SANCTITY OF THE MOTHER'S LIFE

The strength of their conviction was such that pro-life Catholics were prepared to cross the political aisle. But what exactly was their conviction? What did a commitment to the 'sanctity of life' entail? And what did it not entail? And how are we to evaluate this most controversial of principles?

Our starting-point here should be the allegation that the pro-life movement is synonymous with a war on women: that the sanctity of life principle is by definition misogynistic. What are we to make of this claim?

In the 1930s my grandfather, Wilfrid Bardwell Mumford, worked as a GP, a family doctor, in Bermondsey, in the South-East of London – at that time one of the poorest areas in the city. After graduating from Cambridge University with a medical degree, he chose to forgo the cushy life of buying into a medical practice in leafy suburbia. Instead he served families without health insurance, the sort of families who could be slowly bankrupted by an illness such as pneumonia. Then, during the Blitz, when Nazi air strikes flattened London, he administered medical care to working-class patients forced to shelter below ground on the platforms of tube stations. The conditions, as you can imagine, were appalling.

In terms of obstetric care, my grandfather talked about being called out on emergency home visits to find women in obstructed labour. The baby would present head-first, but there was no way the mother's pelvis was going to allow it to pass. The head was simply too big. And typically, at the point my grandfather was called for, it was too late to get the mother to one of the nearest hospitals (St Olave's or Guy's) for an emergency Caesarean section (dangerous in itself, given that he was working in the days before antibiotics). So, in that moment my grandfather faced an immediate decision: either to save the life of the mother by performing a craniotomy and thus allow for the extraction of the newone or, alternatively, to choose not to intervene. The baby wouldn't make it either way, even if my grandfather did not perform the operation. And the operation was permitted by the Infant Life (Preservation) Act of 1929.

What disturbed him most of all was that at the precise moment of the operation there was a chance he might be killing a living foetus. Deprived of technology as he was, he wouldn't be able to know for certain. But it was possible he would be performing an abortion, which was for him a horrifying prospect. This is what he wrote subsequently in his diary:

> Obstetric crises occurred from time to time. I remember on two awful occasions having to perforate because of obstructed labour when there had obviously been inefficient and inadequate ante-natal care: a messy business which I hoped I would never have to do again.

For my grandfather, the principle of the sanctity of life did not entail a universal opposition to abortion. The life of the mother was of paramount, and on these unfortunate occasions greater, importance.

Defensive pro-lifers are quick to make exceptions to their stance on abortion in the case of a threat to the mother's life. They speak as if this is a novel concession. But the campaign, led by doctors, to criminalize abortion in the nineteenth century always insisted on this exception. When American doctors, swayed by the newfound scientific discoveries attesting to an earlier date for the beginning of human life, pushed state legislatures to straightforward opposition to abortion, they were adamant that exceptions be enshrined in law.[4] In 1859 the newly formed American Medical Association condemned the procuring of abortion at every period of gestation, 'except as necessary for preserving the life of either mother or child'. Writing in 1864, Hugh Hodge, a professor of the diseases of women and children at the University of Pennsylvania, made it crystal clear. While abortion is 'one of those unnatural and horrible violations of divine laws', it is also the case that the doctor 'cannot allow the female to perish under his eye when the means of preserving her life is in his power'.[5] The doctors unanimously insisted on a get-out clause when the mother was at risk. A physician at the bedside can't stand back and do nothing when his patient is haemorrhaging blood and her three other children are peeping in to see if their mother is going to be there come the dawn. Consequently, by 1900, of all the states that had outlawed abortion only six did not include provisions for doctors to intervene to preserve the life of the mother.[6]

My point is this: since pro-lifers have been historically averse to sacrificing the life of the mother for that of the child, it is difficult to accuse the movement of literally 'waging a war on women'.

The revolution in obstetric medicine has of course meant that those times, mercifully, are mostly behind us. And yet the pro-choice lobby still charges the pro-life movement with waging a war on women. Why is this? Because, it maintains, the various activities in which the pro-life movement engages are designed subtly to coerce women to have their babies.

What that argument presupposes, however, is that women are not already being coerced. In our extraordinary moment, #MeToo has, finally, exposed the insidious, subtle forms male coercion can take. But often coercion does not stop at sex. One study by the Guttmacher Institute found that, just as some men coerce women to have their children, so others coerce them to abort. One story recounted to the Guttmacher researchers related to a man who had initially wanted a child but, a few months into the pregnancy, changed his mind. He proceeded to punch his 21-year-old partner in the stomach in order to try and induce an abortion, or 'throw her down the staircase if she didn't have one'.

Knowing from past history that his violent threats were real, the woman opted to terminate her pregnancy.[7]

'Abortion', *New York Magazine* observes, 'is something we tend to be more comfortable discussing as an abstraction; the feelings it provokes are too complicated to face in all their particularities.'[8] And the particularities, the report proceeds to demonstrate, all too often have to do with coercion – not just from male partners but also from wider families. This is the testimony of Heather, 32, from Tennessee:

> I already had two daughters. Neither was planned, and it never, ever, occurred to me to terminate those pregnancies. I was brought up with a very religious background. Now I've had two abortions, and if my family knew, my relationship with my family would be gone. My first was two years ago. My husband and I were having financial problems and were considering separating. I just had to shut my conscience down. The doctor was grotesque. He whistled show tunes. I could hear the vacuum sucking out the fetus alongside his whistling. When I hear show tunes now, I shudder. Later, he lost his license. A few months ago, I got pregnant again. My in-laws have been helping us out financially, so we have no choice but to involve them in our decisions. They gave us $500 cash to bring to the clinic. I felt very forced. I felt like I was required to have an abortion to provide for my current family. Money help is a manipulation.

'I felt very forced.' It has been to combat this coercion that crisis pregnancy centres – the institutional backbone of the pro-life movement – have been established since the 1960s. The first international crisis service, Birthright International, was founded by a Canadian woman, Louise Summerhill, motivated by her awareness of the 'acute familial scrutiny of unmarried women experiencing unplanned pregnancies'.[9] The empowerment of women in straitened circumstances, she believed, required more than moral imperatives; women needed practical support. And bereft of funding, Summerhill's operation depended on 'the good hearts and hard work of volunteers'.

Understanding the pro-life movement this way – as essentially countering coercion – makes it harder to sustain the charge that the sanctity of life principle perpetuates a war against women. But if it's not that, what is the sanctity of life really about?

The pro-choice lobby levels another charge at this point: pro-lifers are, at a subconscious level, motivated by fear. What fear? Fear of the decline of traditional *mores*. Fear of complicity with the increasingly liberal spirit of the age. For ever since, in a famous encyclical of 1968, Pope Paul VI refused to relax strictures against the use of contraceptives, for conservative Catholics, opposition to abortion has been joined at the hip with opposition to birth control.

That coincidence of causes is historically important, certainly. Yet to conclude that the sanctity of life is really a last refuge of cultural authority is to attribute to the pro-life movement a false consciousness that seems unwarranted. Consider, for example, what Marjorie Dannenfelser recently told *The New Yorker* about why she set up the nation's foremost national pro-life advocacy group – the Susan B. Anthony List. 'I [go] to sleep thinking, Oh, my gosh, thirty-eight hundred children are going to die tomorrow. What am I going to do to actually save some of them?'[10] Are we really prepared to think Dannenfelser is fooling herself? That we know better than her what drives her? To say that fornication is what *really* roils her seems far-fetched. She believes the newone's life is holy and therefore should be protected at all costs. Maybe she is mistaken about that, but it's clear that is her animating conviction.

'Maybe she is mistaken.' But is she? We can postpone the fundamental question no longer.

THE QUESTION OF VALUE

Perhaps we can approach the vexed question of the status of the newone this way. For defenders of abortion, the debate typically hinges on a supposed distinction between a human being and a person. The newone is unquestionably a human being – a member of the species *homo sapiens* – something that can be determined scientifically, something we can tell by looking at the chromosomes in the cells of living organisms.[11] Further: we can speak about *beginnings* when it comes to human beings. That is, it would be strange to say that 'my father developed himself into me.' No, we can identify an origin. We can point to a radical discontinuity. We can say that a newone comes into existence when a sperm is fused with an ovum (usually) in the ampula of the fallopian tube. That's a matter of fact. But is the newone a person?

Personhood is what philosophers call a *nomen dignitatis* – a 'name of dignity'. Personhood is a way of designating a certain status. 'Person' designates an entity that has value. People count. They matter morally. They are our equals. They belong to us. They are ends in themselves. They can't be treated as mere means. Their interests have to be weighed up. In terms of 'the boundary question', they are in and not out. They warrant legal protection. They have rights, beginning, crucially, with the right to life. Which means you can't wrongfully kill persons. Or sacrifice persons to the greater good. How is it, though, that we decide who is a person? *That* is the question.

Imagine a couple happily expecting. They had been trying for a baby and were duly thrilled to discover they had conceived. They want the baby they've begotten. They desire the child. So at six weeks they listen with delight to the heartbeat. They carefully chart each new phase of development on an App. They sit enthralled and in awe at what appears to them on the ultrasound and stick the print-out on the fridge for all to see. The pregnant woman unhesitatingly talks about herself as a mother. She takes care of herself from the beginning. She stops smoking the moment she realizes she is pregnant. Now she thinks twice about rushing across the street to catch a bus. Both she and her partner think of the new one as a person whose life it would be wrong to terminate.

Imagine now an alternative couple. This couple who did not intend to conceive but find 'they' are pregnant all the same. The contraception failed, in fact. They feel, and not without reason, that they lack the emotional and financial resources to raise what is for them a third child. They do not listen to the heartbeat or see the ultrasound or name the baby. They do not refer to themselves as a mother and a father. They do not think of the new one as a person.

It seems strange to say that a baby is a person if it's wanted, but not a person if it's not. Strange, that is, to say one being's status owes to another being's will. What I find compelling about the conservative position is the affirmation that there is a fact of the matter about value: that value is not subjectively determined. That it's not all a matter of perception. The strength of the conservative position is its acknowledgement of the truth that either the first couple are right to treat their unborn baby as they do or the second couple are. It cannot be both. Either the first couple are projecting their hopes onto the newone in treating it as a person or the second couple are refusing to acknowledge something that is the case. Differently put, either no human beings are people at the earliest stage of their existence or all of them are.

'At the earliest stage of their existence.' The reason I come down on the latter view – that all human beings are persons – is because, ultimately, I think it corresponds more adequately to the way the world is. We are not creatures who appear in the world as in the Greek or Hebrew myths – full-bodied, standing on our own two feet, rational and ready to go. On the contrary, we grow over time in the bodies of other members of our kind, the first stage of our existence a state of radical dependency. Any attempt to say that at point x in pregnancy a human being becomes a person – with the onset of consciousness, say, whenever that is – ignores the phenomenon of human development, the gradual manner of our emergence. We are precious from the start.

THE COST OF FREEDOM

The Sanctity of Life principle – the belief that a newone is a person whose life should therefore be protected at all costs – is what determines the Right's opposition to abortion. It is this value which mobilizes millions of Americans to do all they can to promote a culture of life. Having established that, we are now in a position to tackle the central question of this chapter: how would we expect a commitment to the sanctity of life to play out when it comes to the debate over gun control?

The way of life that conservatives feel is endangered by gun control was recently on display at a youth marksmanship competition at Camp Perry, Ohio. 'People say how good I did in the match, how I won the trophy, won the rifle, all that ... but really the guy who won the match was God. I was just a body pulling the trigger.' These are the words of the 15-year-old Robert McClain from Walkersville, West Virginia, who won the tournament. McClain was firing an AR-15 without sights at a distance of 200 yards. He secured a score of 390-4x, beating 600 fellow-shooters – an astonishing achievement for a contestant who had only begun shooting the year previously. His coach, Dick Whiting, fully expects him to be classified as a High Master in less than two years.[12]

A sport, then, like any other; a sport involving great skill, requiring intense practice. 'I just took my time and squeezed all my shots,' Robert McClain explained. But isn't the sport potentially dangerous? Again, like any other. But when regulated, perfectly safe. Competitions like this are an integral part of community life. The fact that the gun is semi-automatic, a firearm that automatically reloads, is immaterial. That's what made McClain's tournament all the more competitive.

At 9.34 on a bone-chilling December morning a troubled 20-year-old decided to drop in on his old elementary school and pay them a visit. He came with an AR-15 semi-automatic rifle made by Bushmaster, and ten magazines holding 30 rounds each. Dressed in black camouflage and a military-style vest, wearing yellow earplugs and with an empty camouflage drop holster affixed to his right thigh, he arrived at the locked school entrance. In less than a second he unloaded six .223 calibre bullets into a plate glass window. He stepped over the shards of glass, walking on through the breach he had made. He strode down the corridors he knew like the back of his hand, vivid adolescent memories clinging to every corner. He entered a first-grade classroom, where he found a substitute teacher shielding 16 six- and seven-year-old pupils behind her. Adam Lanza unloaded his semi-automatic and within seconds the teacher and 14 of her students were dead. Another was to die in hospital. 'Mommy, I'm OK, but all my friends are dead,' said the sole survivor, a six-year-old girl. Before he took his own life, Adam Lanza had fired 154 rounds from the rifle in less than ten minutes, with some of the slain children riddled with as many as 11 bullets. He committed suicide the moment the first police officer arrived on the scene.

Lanza could commit this deadly school massacre solely because of the weapon he had in his possession. In the ten minutes between entering the school and the arrival of the police a simple rifle would have allowed him to release fewer rounds.

Robert McClain and Adam Lanza used the same weapon. The freedom that allowed Robert McClain to win an innocent marksmanship competition in rural Ohio allowed Adam Lanza to commit his horrific crime.

Despite the depressing frequency of gun massacres, the Right's opposition to gun control today is implacable and historically anomalous.* The organization Gun Owners of America declares, 'Gun control has no place in a free society.' The Arizona Citizens Defense League states it was established because 'the image of freedom in Arizona doesn't match reality'. 'For Freedom' is how the President of the National Association for Gun Rights signs off his newsletters. And according to the National Rifle Association, 'There is one thing that NRA members and law-abiding gun owners must proudly take responsibility for – the preservation of the rights that secure our liberty. And to do that, we must once again organize and inform others of the danger to our freedom and way of life.'

The collateral consequences of this way of life are evident:

America is absolutely awash with easily obtainable firearms. You can go down to a gun show at the local convention centre and come away with a fully automatic assault rifle, without a background check, and most likely without having to show an identification card.[13]

So wrote an al-Qaeda operative. Adam Gadahn went on to exhort jihadists to take advantage of lax American

---

* The possession of guns had always coexisted with gun restrictions. Astonishingly, the first President of the NRA, Karl T. Frederick, a 1920 Olympic gold-medal winner for marksmanship, had an instinctive distaste for 'the general practice of carrying weapons'. In response to the prohibition-era havoc wrought by machine-gun wielding gangsters such as Al Capone and desperadoes like John Dillinger and Bonnie and Clyde, President Franklin Delano Roosevelt moved to pass the first Federal gun control bill. Karl Frederick testified in its defence: 'I do not believe in the general promiscuous toting of guns.' Hardly to be considered a raving liberal, even Ronald Regan opposed the promiscuous toting of guns. In 1967, when he was governor of California, he declared, 'There's no reason why on the street today a citizen should be carrying loaded weapons.'

gun culture: 'What are you waiting for?' It's not just the presence of bad guys like him, but also the availability of guns that puts people's lives at risk – the terrorist dared to question the mantra. America has around 4 per cent of the world's population but almost half of its civilian-owned guns. Its firearm homicide rate is about 20 times the average among OECD countries excluding Mexico. Even sites such as usconservative.com freely admit that 'it's common sense to know that, yes, the United States will probably have more gun murders than a country with almost no guns and no households with guns.'[14]

To focus on internal terrorism, of course, is to give a warped picture of the cost of freedom. Assault weapons account for only a fraction of fatalities. The reason gun deaths in the US have risen to their highest rates in 20 years is because of the rise in suicides involving firearms, accounting for 60 per cent of the almost 40,000 fatal shootings annually.

As tragic as suicides, moreover, are accidents. 'It's something that didn't need to happen,' concluded Capt. David Angelo in the press conference. Two-year-old Christopher Williams – 'Junior' – had found his father's 9mm handgun in the living-room couch. His parents were both at home. When his devastated father was led out of his home in handcuffs, all he could do was cry and yell, 'He was my son.'[15]

One promising proposal to reverse this trend is the introduction of smart guns – weapons activated by PIN-coded wristwatches, locks that can be inserted into barrels, technology that uses biometrics to unlock triggers. In a stroke, firearms could be rendered useless to young children, suicidal teenagers, thieves. (The inventor of one model, Omer Kiyani, has been developing his design ever since he was shot in the face as a teenager.)

The fact that more children in the US are killed by firearms than by cancer came as a surprise to me.[16] It shouldn't have, considering there are guns in one in three American households with children.[17] Furthermore, while the rate of car-related deaths has halved since the beginning of the twenty-first century, there has been no progress at all in terms of firearm injuries.[18]

It is difficult to see why anyone committed to the sanctity of life would oppose the development of such smart gun technology. The NRA, however, *has* objected, issuing a recent statement that, though they have no problem with smart guns *per se*, they take issue with a mandate requiring gun dealers *only* to sell smart guns. 'The choice should be left to the marketplace.'

A WAY OF LIFE

Gun control is a weapon that coastal elites use to try and destroy a way of rural life they don't like or understand. That is the argument. A Washington cabal is trying to impose its will on huge swathes of the country whose politics happen to be radically different. Why should law-abiding Americans who farm the plains and hunt the mountain forests have their freedom to use a *tool* curtailed by what happens in cities they'll never visit, or in states that could not be more remote?

'If I had gotten off an hour earlier,' 23-year-old Anthony Lipford said, kicking himself in the leg with frustration, 'I would have been here.' At four o'clock on a Friday afternoon his daughter, McKenzie Elliott, a three-year-old African-American girl he described as 'vibrant, with energy out of this world', was sitting on a neighbour's porch in the North Baltimore's Waverly neighbourhood. Suddenly a car raced up Old York Road and halted at the intersection of East 36th Street. Someone inside opened fire at a person standing on the corner, who in turn returned fire. McKenzie was caught in the crossfire. A stray bullet flew across four homes along from the street corner to the porch the child was sitting on. She died that day. As one resident put it, 'Evil has visited our community and taken the life of an innocent child.'[19]

Rural Americans may well be right about the elite's disdain for their way of life. That doesn't change the fact that often it's their fellow citizens in the inner cities who bear the cost. Turf wars in Compton, drive-by shootings in New York, initiation ceremonies on the south side of Chicago: gang violence is an urban phenomenon. And it is no respecter of people, spilling over into the streets of the poorest neighbourhoods in the US, taking the lives of innocent children like McKenzie Elliott. It takes the lives of young Hispanic and black men. Among young African-Americans gun homicide is currently the leading cause of death, and blacks are six times as likely as whites to be the victims of a homicide.

The CEO of the National Sports Shooting Federation recently expressed his indignation at the promotion of gun control in these terms: 'Millions of law-abiding sportsmen across the nation own [assault rifles], and when those misinformed about firearms say that "no sportsman has any need for a gun that is only used to kill people," they are in effect calling millions of American sportsmen murderers.'[20] When you take your AR-15 to shoot rabbits on your property, you're not intending to do anything to someone you consider to be a person.

Yet what does it mean to belong to a citizenry? Unless borders are to be introduced between states, it makes no sense to have one law about guns for one state and another law for another. This means the individual, or the sub-group, is obliged to take into account the concerns of the whole country. They cannot exempt themselves from the advisability of a policy for the nation, which it is their duty to shape. To do so is in fact to secede from the responsibility of self-governing and to fail to acknowledge the bonds of connection between one's fellow-countrymen. The part cannot relinquish responsibility for the whole.

Further, to take responsibility for the whole means to take seriously at any given moment the flawed reality of the country you find yourself in. In an ideal world weapons would only be in the hands of responsible users intending them for recreational purposes. But the reality of self-rule means disavowing the utopian blindness that says this is the case. Guns designed for recreational purposes will find their way into the hands of the wrong people.[21]

SELF-DEFENCE AND SNAP JUDGEMENTS

The Right's resistance to gun control demonstrates a wavering commitment to the sanctity of life. Yet is there not a glaring oversight in my argument? The central purpose of having and bearing arms, many gun owners insist, is self-defence. Set aside cynicism about the gun lobby's underlying commercial interests. It remains the case, says the gun lobby, that saving lives is what the freedom to wield firearms is for. Which makes the real question whether the number of lives *lost* due to the availability of guns in America is greater than the number of lives *saved* by their availability.

It is this argument that underpins the predictability of the gun lobby's response to gun massacres. After one horrendous school massacre, the NRA President declared, 'The only way to stop a monster from killing our kids is to be personally involved and invested in a plan of absolute protection.'[22] And Donald Trump, in the wake of the shooting in Parkland, Florida, proposed arming 20 per cent of teachers across America's 135,000 schools.[23]

In his fascinating book *Blink*, Malcolm Gladwell analyses the phenomenon of 'snap judgements', the split-second decisions we make to intervene in crisis situations. Gladwell's primary case is the police's shooting of Amadou Diallo in the South Bronx, New York City. When officers saw a black man, Diallo, take out of his coat a shiny dark object, they assumed it was a gun. They shot him 41 times. But when they inspected his body in the hallway of his apartment they realized it was a wallet he was reaching for. With the adrenalin pumping and cortisol rushing, the officers made snap decisions. The situation, and their predilection to return fire, impaired their judgement. The outcome was devastating.[24]

In another case, on a busy Saturday night in Times Square, a man was walking erratically through oncoming traffic. Again the police thought he was reaching into his pocket for a gun. So they fired three shots. One buried itself into the knee of a 54-year-old woman. Another grazed a second woman. Not one hit the target.

These were trained police officers, professionals trying to do the job they had been taught to do. They failed abysmally. In the heat of the moment, the judgement of even the brightest and the best can be impaired.

Now imagine untrained janitors stationed in schools invaded by a homicidal kid. Imagine the adrenalin and cortisol rushing, the snap judgements, the split-second responses. Bullets ricocheting into the bodies of children? Shoot-outs in corridors lined by lockers? Sick mass killers getting to play *Call of Duty* for real? Even further, logically, if you are going to place armed officers in schools, what weapons should they have? Surely if they are going to match Adam Lanza's AR-15, you can't rest content with giving mere handguns to school law enforcement personnel? They will need assault rifles too. And so we presage the proliferation of weapons. An arms race.

Another part of the conservative plan of absolute protection is more gun-free zones and more permit holders carrying their arms with them at all times. And again, after the shooting in Emanuel African Methodist Episcopal Church in Charleston, South Carolina, the Gun Owners of America bemoaned the fact that the slain pastor, Rev. Clementa Pinckney, had not been armed during the Bible study at the end of which 21-year-old Dylann Roof opened fire. If every pastor in every church in the US had a handgun strapped to his belt, more lives would be saved is the thesis.

If trained policemen so often make fateful snap judgements, how about untrained citizens? How would the even greater proliferation of weapons not lead to an escalation of violence? Would the mass armament of the citizenry, millions more entering the fray, lead to more or fewer people being caught by stray bullets? Maybe the only thing worse than one bad guy with a gun would be lots of good guys with guns.

Engaging in the enterprise of assigning blame for the terrible outbreaks of violence in a civilized society, the Right squarely lays the blame at Hollywood's door. As one conservative critic puts it: 'They [liberals] have an entertainment industry that makes billions of dollars by glorifying violence in film, music, graphic novels, and video games, and then piously lecture the rest of the country on the evils of guns and the NRA.'[25] The point is well taken. When it comes to public shootings, by glorifying violence Hollywood has a lot to answer for. But hasn't Hollywood also inspired amateurs to believe that, if a ghastly shoot-out were to break out in the mall, they would coolly take down their targets rather than, clenching Baby Glocks in perspiring palms, misfire into innocent bystanders? Does not the self-defence argument hinge on that self-deceit? Is there not a temptation in a macho culture to overestimate one's ability to be a hero when the time comes?

A CULTURE OF LIFE

During the 2016 Republican primary, one presidential candidate laid out the terms of the gun debate with remarkable candour: 'I never saw a body with bullet holes that was more devastating than taking the right to arm ourselves away.'[26] The loss of life owing to guns may be tragic, but worse would be the loss of the liberty to have guns. Gun violence is the inevitable cost of freedom.

Such a sentiment, I have argued, flies in the face of a commitment to the sanctity of life. The consistent application of the Talmudic conviction that 'he who saves one life saves the world entire' would see the Right doing everything within their power to restrict the availability of lethal weapons.

5

REVERENCE FOR NATURE: WHY GREENS SHOULDN'T BECOME CYBORGS

When I was at university, tucked away on a thousand-year-old side-street, there existed a little organization with a preposterous name – the Future of Humanity Institute. In that office sat a lonely philosopher playing out various scenarios in his mind about what happens next to the species, nay, the planet, nay, the galaxy. Humanity conquers death. Humanity conquers Mars. Technology conquers humanity etc. etc.

At least, I am now told he did. None of us had ever heard of him at the time. None of us encountered the Future of Humanity Institute, despite our vested interest in it. Nick Bostrom didn't feature in the student newspapers. He didn't have a stall at Freshers' Fair. Bostrom was hidden away like other obscure academics, whiling away the time on quixotic questions – even more off the map since he didn't teach undergraduates.

Today, however, the movement in which Bostrom is a luminary – transhumanism – is in the ascendant. Its self-avowed aim is to 'seek the continuation and acceleration of the intelligent life beyond its currently human form and human limitations by means of science and technology'.[1] The cult has gone public. Its home has migrated from an attic operation in a quiet college town to the shiny giant complexes of Silicon Valley. A crazy coterie of utopians connected by the internet, signing charters and committing themselves to 'The Principles of Extropy', has come to the attention of the world. How on earth has this happened?

One reason for transhumanism's sudden prominence is the staggering development of Artificial Intelligence (AI) during the last decade. The breakthrough in Deep Learning – the machine learning technique that mimics the brain mechanisms by which we identify patterns in large amounts of data – has precipitated astonishing advances. Robots have come along by leaps and bounds. Long-lasting records in speech and language recognition have been smashed almost overnight. And the quicker the discoveries have come, the more urgent the question has become: 'How long would it be until an artificial intelligence could reason indistinguishably from a human being?'[2] Inevitably, AI researchers and big-tech have come knocking on the door of the transhumanists, inviting them to their conferences, joining with foundations to pour fortunes into their research projects.[3]

Meanwhile, while robots stride forth from laboratories on one side of the corridor, from a laboratory on the other side has emerged the world's first designer baby. As I wrestle with words and struggle with syntax, news has just come in of the delivery of a genetically edited child. A Chinese scientist claims to have successfully modified the germline, deleting at embryo stage a gene that acts as a 'doorway' to HIV infection, and bringing twins to term. For the first time, the constitution of a human being and all its descendants will have been altered by another human being. The aim of this endeavour may be to cure disease, the final goal of medicine. But for transhumanists this is not the end but the beginning – a baby step towards the enhancement of human faculties and the self-transformation of human nature. They dream of one day enabling parents to enhance the cognitive capabilities of their children to fit them better to the challenges of a very different world.

———

Inclusivity – concern for the marginalized. *Sufficiency* – contentment with what we have. We have so far in this book identified and affirmed two fundamental principles on the Left. And we have seen the positions on assisted dying and sexual consumerism which, I believe, those values entail. In this chapter I want to turn to a third value – *reverence* – which is expressed so clearly in the Left's attitude towards the environment. I want to explore transhumanism in light of this value. What would be an environmentalist take on proposals radically to enhance human beings?

What is the justification, you might ask, for running together environmentalism and transhumanism? In preceding chapters the particular pairings of positions within the package deals should hopefully have been clear. The respective debates about abortion and gun control are both about life. Or, given the strong things the Left has historically had to say about consumerism, the phenomenon of *sexual* consumerism demands that we think simultaneously about the Left's view of sexual liberation. Why run together climate change with human genetic enhancement? The answer has to do with the *altered nature of human action*. We may not be able to control the consequences we unleash through our moral decisions, but we typically expect the vicissitudes of history to bring about some kind of reversion. Now, though, in respect to both the future of the planet and the future of the species, we are in a different situation. Now the nature of human action is radically altered since the decisions we make could well prove irreversible. How, then, are we to go about understanding our responsibilities? Which direction(s) to head in? Which paths to rule out?

REVERENCE FOR NATURE

Concern for the environment was not initially high on the agenda of the burgeoning ranks of the young radicals of the 1960s. Two years after its founding, in 1962, the Students for a Democratic Society organization (SDS) published its seminal 'Port Huron Statement'. Of burning concern: the country's military-industrial complex, the racial bigotry that blighted society, labour relations, the legacy of colonialism, the threat of nuclear annihilation. In dozens of pages the environment received only a single sentence: a vague reference to the threat of overpopulation.

A number of lone activists were convinced this could change. In September 1969 Gaylord Nelson, a Democratic senator from Wisconsin, declared: 'I am convinced that the same concern the youth of this nation took in changing this nation's priorities on the war in Vietnam and on civil rights can be shown for the problem of the environment.'[4] A year later, wielding the most recent scientific revelations about environmentalist degradation, and tapping into the Left's predisposition to question the effects of industrial capitalism, Nelson pulled off one of the largest mass protests in US history. Earth Day 1970 saw 20 million Americans take to the streets to take action on pollution and raise environmental issues to public consciousness.

What was the value to which the leaders of the nascent movement appealed? How did they rally the counterculture to a new cause? As Nelson's colleague and Earth Day coordinator Barry Hayes put it, looking back: 'We hoped it would lead to a new kind of ideology, a new value system based on ecology and a reverence for life.'[5]

Since then, reverence has remained the foundational principle for the Left, the preferred nomenclature of environmentalists across the world – from local wildlife conservationist chapters to radical 'ecotage' operatives to international bodies. When the historic Earth Charter was drawn up in 1990, it climaxed with the words: 'Let ours be a time remembered for the awakening of a new reverence for life, the firm resolve to achieve sustainability, the quickening of the struggle for justice and peace, and the joyful celebration of life.'[6]

What is meant by 'reverence'? There are, of course, a hundred different ways in which a hundred different organizations can utilize a concept like reverence. Is it impossibly amorphous? Can we speak here of a stable, shared meaning of this organizing principle?

reverence. *n.* a feeling or attitude of deep respect tinged with awe; veneration

Other synonyms for 'reverence' include 'wonder', 'admiration' and 'honour'. Those words pick out in the

first instance what we might call *aesthetic receptivity*.
As in:

> The sounding cataract
> Haunted me like a passion: the tall rock,
> The mountain, and the deep and gloomy wood,
> Their colours and their forms, were then to me
> An appetite; a feeling and a love ...[7]

When the Romantic poets exhorted their public to revere
nature, they were exhorting them to pay attention. For
they knew how easy it is to pass by 'these beauteous
forms'. They knew we can fail to see the trees for the
wood. We can ignore the fire and the rose, remain deaf
to the bird that 'singest of summer in full-throated ease'.
And the cost of our irreverence, in this aesthetic sense, is
the diminishment of our lives.

'Aesthetic receptivity', though, does not carry the
weight of the word as environmentalists employ it. For
environmentalists, 'reverence' is not a recommendation.
It is a demand. It denotes the attitude proper to the
reality of our situation. It is the posture prescribed by
the way the world is. Whereas the Romantics are saying,
'The world is beautiful, and if you fail to see that, you
lose out,' the environmental movement demands, 'the
world is such that it ought to be treated with respect.'

Our existence depends on the equilibrium and stability
of the biosphere. We are not astronauts who have fitted
out the place for habitation. We exist on a planet that
produced vitality before we arrived on the scene. The
intricacy of the natural order, the web of interactions
between species and between species and the physical
environment – we do not just look upon this as a

beautiful tapestry made by someone else, which it might be wrong to violate.[8] No, this tapestry is the condition for our existence. We wouldn't be here, and we wouldn't be sustained, without it. What we encounter is greater than us, which should elicit a certain humility, but we are also dependent on this greatness, which should elicit a certain gratitude, a certain reverence.

If reverence is the attitude the natural world demands, what follows precisely in terms of our actions? What is the application? What forms of treating nature does this attitude permit, proscribe, require? Does reverence for nature rule out any encroachment whatsoever? For how could this possibly be workable? Surely our survival depends on our not leaving nature as we found it. You don't have to be exposed to the elements for too long to acknowledge that if we had not changed our habitat in all manner of ways, we simply would not have made it as a species.

It is here that the concept of cultivation proves crucial. Cultivation names a symbiosis, an ability to act in concert with nature. The earliest farmers in the Levant conscripted the forces of natural selection to grow the plants they wanted. They drew on organic processes to select crops. In this way they realized potentialities latent in nature. They honoured the patterns of fertility. For ten thousand years human beings have altered their environments by way of agriculture, but they lived within the regenerative capacity of the biosphere.

Cultivation, I think, names a form of engagement with the natural world that is reverent. For it entails the acceptance of limits. What emerges from billions of years of evolution is astonishing complexity, to ignore which requires acts of supreme hubris. For altogether different from cultivation is the picture of what we might call 'mastery'.

MASTERY OF NATURE

Francis Bacon was very excited. The seventeenth-century English statesman writes with palpable euphoria about the most recent technological advances cropping up around him – printing, gunpowder, the compass. 'What a change have these three things made in the world in these times; the one in state of learning, the other in state of war, the third in the state of treasure, commodities, and navigation!'[9] The possibilities for humankind had been thrown wide open. What's more, he observed, these technologies had been stumbled upon by chance. What if people deliberately sought technological breakthroughs? What could be achieved then? What if humankind revised the whole way it related to nature?

It was because of his commitment to this revision that a man who never really invented anything became the father of a technological revolution. Bacon sought to set out a philosophy, to inculcate a new paradigm, to realize the practical possibilities of scientific research. Here's the heart of it:

> The sovereignty of man lieth hid in knowledge; wherein many things are reserved ... now we govern nature but in opinions, but we are in thrall unto her in necessity: but if we would be led by her in invention, we should command her by action.[10]

The picture is one of domination, of mastery. The knowledge Bacon refers to is thoroughly instrumental.

Using nature is for him the giddy new possibility and the great new challenge. The hope for technology (for 'invention') is that, through it, man can finally subject the world to his will, to command her (rather than being 'in thrall unto her in necessity').

In the twentieth century the New Left – in particular, its guru Herbert Marcuse – assailed this worldview. Preceding the development of technology, Marcuse observed, is a projection of nature as the 'stuff of control and organization' and the re-conception of the earth as, again, merely raw material for human purposes and projects, to be utilized and then disposed of.[11]

This, then, is the intellectual paradigm that Bacon inculcated. What of its practical outworking in our world?

Consider how the mastery mindset is demonstrated in agriculture. The vast monocultures of East Anglia or Kansas attest to the eschewing of cultivation in favour of extraction. Intensive farming represents the abandonment of any attempt to imitate natural processes. And we have operated under the illusion that all this may be done indefinitely without detrimental consequences, the illusion that we can somehow possess those materials safely.[12] Soil erosion demonstrates what happens when complex ecosystems are rendered merely 'natural resources', as future fertility is sacrificed for present productivity.

And global warming, too, is testament to the illusion of our dominion. We have literally treated the earth as a source of raw material for our purposes, but we have not got away with it. Our attempts at mastery have been extraordinary; they have also been unsuccessful. 'There was no final conquest, no dominion established', writes David Wallace-Wells in *The Uninhabitable Earth*: 'In fact, the opposite ... with global warming we have unwittingly claimed ownership of a system beyond our ability to control or tame in any day-to-day way.'[13]

THE MASTERY OF HUMAN NATURE

Reverence, then, is a foundational principle for the Left, clearly expressed in its position on the environment. Cultivation is consonant with that value. Mastery eschews it. But what is the fate of this principle when it comes to the ascendant movement that is transhumanism?

Transhumanists could never be accused of being bashful about their beliefs. They don't downplay their vaulting ambitions. Consider one of the founding documents of transhumanism, a 'Letter to Mother Nature' written in 1990 by Max More. In the letter More issues a major complaint. 'You [Mother Nature] have in many ways done a poor job with the human constitution', he objects, before announcing 'it is time to amend [it].'

These are his suggestions:

Amendment No. 1
We will no longer tolerate the tyranny of ageing and death. Through genetic alterations, cellular manipulations, synthetic organs and any necessary means, we will endow ourselves with enduring vitality and remove our expiration date. We will each decide for ourselves how long we shall live.

Amendment No. 2
We will expand our perceptual range through biotechnological and computational means. We seek to exceed the perpetual abilities of any other creature ...

Amendment No. 3
We will improve on our neural organization and capacity, expanding our working memory and enhancing our intelligence.

Amendment No. 4
We will supplement the neo-cortex with a 'meta-brain'. This distributed network of sensors, information processes and intelligence will increase our degree of self-awareness and allow us to modulate our emotions.

Amendment No. 5
We will no longer be slaves to our genes. We will take charge over our genetic programming and achieve mastery over our biological and neurological processes. We will fix all individual and species defects left over from evolution by natural selection. Not content with that, we will seek complete choice of our bodily form and function, refining and augmenting our physical and intellectual abilities beyond those of any human in history.

Amendment No. 6
We will cautiously yet boldly reshape our motivational patterns and emotional responses ...

Amendment No. 7
... We will not limit our physical, intellectual or emotional capacities by remaining purely biological organisms. While we pursue mastery of our own biochemistry, we will increasingly integrate our advancing technologies into ourselves.[14]

'Not content with that ...' The first thing to note about this manifesto is its overwhelming sense of dissatisfaction. Mr More is dissatisfied with the human constitution even in its healthiest state, at the zenith of its development. He is dissatisfied with our genetic programming and neural organization, our perceptual abilities and physical capacities, our motivational patterns and emotional responses. They are simply not good enough. The deliveries of evolution do not suffice. Instead they all require radical enhancement, not just to bring everyone to the level of the optimally functioning human being but, far beyond that, to 'exceed ... every other creature'.

We saw how in the Baconian view nature is construed as merely raw material to be used by human beings, as natural resources to be utilized. Well, now it has come full circle. Now it is us who are being construed as raw material. More's letter explicitly employs the language of 'mastery'. For Bacon, the hope for 'invention' is that, through it, people can finally subject the world to their wills. For More, the hope for invention – for genetic alterations, cellular manipulations, synthetic organs – is to subject ourselves to our will, to take our own evolution in hand, to take charge of our development.

I argued above that mastery is the alternative posture towards nature to reverence. Mr More's letter thus betrays, in both its sense of dissatisfaction and its impulse to mastery, a lack of reverence for human nature – for the given state in which human beings are found, for the kind of creatures we are. (More has admitted as much elsewhere, claiming that 'transhumanists regard human nature not as an end in itself ... having [no] claim on our allegiance.'[15]) Our next task is to explore more fully the way certain enhancements fail to revere human nature and how, if there is a connection between our nature and our good, such enhancements would threaten our good. The first species of enhancement to consider are those which seek to do away with the body; the second, enhancements that upset the mind; the third, enhancements that numb the heart. Let's take these in turn.

TRANSCENDING THE BODY

One historic enthusiast for the internet, John Perry Barlow, once wrote of 'the electronic frontier' that it is 'a world that is both everywhere and nowhere, but it is not where bodies live'.[16] Evidence of his perspicacity is our talk today of 'living online'. Yet for transhumanists this is only the beginning. The 'promise' of brain-machine interfaces is to realize Barlow's vision fully. 'Neural-lace' technology – implanting electrodes into the brain for direct computing capabilities (an iteration of which is already in use for patients with brain injuries) – will, we are told, eventually give us the power literally to plug ourselves in to the internet, to be caught up in the worldwide web. What are we to make of this?

In his wonderfully rich book *The World Beyond Your Head* Matthew Crawford presents *attention* as a fundamental human good, as one of the things flourishing humans do. Certain skilled practices are valuable, he argues, because by training our powers of concentration we allow external things to 'pull us out of ourselves'. When we cook a meal for a big occasion, for example, answers to the questions of 'What is to be done next?' are located 'outside our own heads, in relation to objects and other people'.[17] We have to subject ourselves to the constraints of the circumstances. Once we have set about a project of this kind, we can't just do what we like. We zero in on the task to hand, attuning ourselves to the environment.

A precondition of attention is embodiment. In the standard view, perception is merely a deduction our brain performs – a purely mental process in which my mind takes the equivalent of a still photograph and then undertakes a kind of 3D modelling to achieve 'the rounded-out sense we have of the world'.[18] The reality, however, is that we think through our bodies. Cognition, far more than we care to admit, depends on our ability to move around an object and see what is the same or different about it from various perspectives. This alternative view puts us back in the world. What we *do* is central to how we *see*.

Attention depends on embodiment in another way too. To attend to something is to select; to pick out one item from the flux of things is by definition to screen off others. And the principle of selection is determined by our situatedness – where we are physically located offers a default reason to attend to a certain object or person we encounter. Those phenomena which are 'within reach' and 'to hand' take priority by sheer virtue of this co-presence.

A life lived virtually, however, 'removes us from whatever situation we inhabit directly', eradicating physical co-presence and making us as near or as far from things and people as we choose. How do we then select what to pay attention to? There is no longer a default answer given by our actual frame of reference. Crawford speaks of a 'uniform distancelessness'. Taking a virtual tour of the Forbidden City in Beijing, or deep underwater caverns, is as easy as looking across the room. But this constitutes a crisis. For, he writes,

> ... where am I? There doesn't seem to be any nonarbitrary basis on which I can draw a horizon around myself – a zone of relevance – by which I might take my bearings and get oriented. When the axis of closer-to-me and farther-from-me is collapsed, I can be anywhere, and find that I am rarely in any place in particular. To be present with those I share a life with is then one option among many ...[19]

The introduction of brain-machine interfaces (or even whole-brain emulation[20]), in its ambition to double down on virtual reality, will entrench these pathologies. By transcending the body even more radically, we will further diminish human experience.

UPSETTING THE MIND

Transcending the body constitutes a failure to revere human nature, to accept the limits that condition our flourishing. That is our first contention. A second set of enhancements proposed by transhumanists threaten to upset the mind.

Transhumanists imagine various routes towards 'superintelligence'. First, psychopharmacology. We are already aware of the efficacy of 'smart drugs' to improve concentration. What would happen if it became a matter of course to boost the cognitive power of people *without* attention deficit disorders?

Next, science-fiction writers and transhumanists have long dreamt of genetic manipulation as a means towards superintelligence. As genome-wide trait analysis becomes more sophisticated, and epigenetic factors better understood, parents might be able to select for strongly heritable traits such as IQ at embryo stage, or even make their embryos to order via the synthesizing of genomes, designing a child with a specific combination of their genetic inputs.

Those are the potential technological means. What about the cultural shift required? What would it take to whet people's appetite for cognitive enhancement?

Focusing on genetic manipulation, we can imagine how cognitive enhancement might fall out of the logic of procreative freedom. Consider what James Watson said on the 50th anniversary of his co-discovery of the structure of DNA:

> I am against society imposing rules on individuals for how they want to use genetic knowledge. Just let people decide what they want to do. Parents ... should be allowed to decide whether or not to have a child with Down's syndrome, or in the future an enhanced one. Anything – a short child, a tall child, an aggressive child ... I'm for using genetics at the level of the individual ... It's best to let people try and do what they think best. I wouldn't want someone

else to tell me what to do – as long as you are not hurting someone else.[21]

Imagine how this might happen. It starts with IVF and the testing of the embryo for chromosomal abnormalities. We already select against embryos and foetuses on an industrial scale. But why should we stop with fertilizing one egg, particularly if stem cell technologies provide us with an endless supply? So, we make a habit of selecting the very best embryos, the most suitable candidates. But what if all of them are found to be defective? Perhaps by that time the technology to replace the faulty genes will be to hand. But why go through the rigmarole of swapping out genes if you can edit them directly? Would amending genes be so different an intervention from replacing them? And if you're going to amend genes to prevent disease, why not, while you're at it, amend genes to prevent disadvantage? Why not give your child the best start in life – by boosting their immune system, or even enhancing their memory? And if you're going to give your child the best start in life, and the ability to cope with the complexities of the late twenty-first century, why wouldn't you attempt to gift them greater intelligence?

And we're there. As Yuval Noah Harari writes perceptively:

Healing is the initial justification for every upgrade. Find some professors experimenting in genetic engineering or brain-computer interfaces, and ask them why they are engaged in such research. 'With the help of genetic engineering,' they would explain, 'we could defeat cancer ...' Maybe, but it will surely not end there

... Once you achieve a momentous breakthrough, you cannot restrict its use to healing and complexity and completely forbid it for upgrading.[22]

What would it be like if this future were brought into being? We can imagine societal consequences – the formation of class divisions greater than the ones we have today between the educated and uneducated. But at the level of the individual – our focus here – what would cognitive enhancement portend?

We can get a grip on our question by asking first, 'What exactly is it that transhumanists propose to enhance?' Intelligence, we are told. But what type of intelligence? The more one reads the transhumanists, the more striking appears the reduction of intelligence to computation or 'calculative rationality' – the ability to retrieve, sift and apply information. But what about all the other forms of intelligence? Does calculative rationality really exhaust the domain of mental activity?

What is the effect of reducing intelligence to computation? Recall what we said about the meaning of reverence. For environmentalists what demands reverence is the equilibrium that makes our terrestrial life possible. Taking a holistic view allows us to identify the extraordinary alignment of factors that allows this world to be our home. And we are only too aware of what happens when this balance is upset. Well, in the same way, if the 'candidate' for enhancement is only one form of intelligence, what we have to fear is that the exaggeration or accentuation of this one form will upset the given balance between the different forms of intelligence that make up our minds.

Calculative rationality, as Nick Bostrom is happy to concede, is typically understood as means-ends (or instrumental) reasoning. If instrumental reason is enhanced – which is the proposal – we are told that executing a given task will become radically quicker, radically more efficient. But that begs the question of how one decides what ends to choose to pursue in the first place, and that requires a different form of intelligence – what in the classical philosophical tradition we might call 'deliberative rationality' or even wisdom – the ability to weigh up options, to discriminate, to judge, to step back from our desires, to select our priorities, to discern our vocations, to think what we are doing. The improvement of concentration will not necessarily increase wisdom. On the contrary, we have reason to fear one form of intelligence would eclipse another.

NUMBING THE HEART

To transcend the body. To upset the mind. To these two failures of reverence to human nature we must add a third: the threat transhumanist proposals pose to our *hearts*.

Vulnerability derives from the Latin for 'wound' (*vulnus*). We are woundable creatures. My friend betrays my trust. I'm left exposed by former intimacy. My partner knows me well enough to hit where it hurts. And our sensitivity concusses us. How much more could we accomplish if we were thick-skinned?

Yet while our agency is impaired by our vulnerability, we are nevertheless rightly suspicious of the dictum 'sticks and stones may break my bones but words will never hurt me'. If a person is impervious to emotion, we sense something is up. We wonder why. We wonder what's wrong. We look to excavate what it is in their past that makes them so resilient, so dysfunctional.

Consider grief. The openness to another required for love necessarily makes one vulnerable to heartbreak.[23] Someone who is unaffected, who remains stoical or moves on quickly, whose mood stabilizes straight away – we would either question the person, as above, or we would question the depth of the love. But if we are given to love and to be loved, if that comes with the territory of living a flourishing human life, then we must say that vulnerability does too.

Now, given the indispensable place of vulnerability, it is particularly important to question another form of alteration that transhumanists propose: mood enhancements.

'A merry little surge of electricity piped by automatic alarm from the mood organ beside his bed awakened Rick Deckard.' Thus opens the novel that became the film *Blade Runner*, Philip K. Dick's novel *Do Androids Dream of Electric Sheep?* The amusing scene which ensues sees Deckard and his wife discussing the various moods they wish to induce in themselves by recourse to these mood organs. For example: 'At his console he hesitated between dialling for a thalamic suppressant (which would abolish his mood of rage) or a thalamic stimulant (which would make him feel irked enough to win the argument).'

The spectre of such sophisticated mood control is haunting for the reason that we are so averse to the kind of vulnerability which, we saw, makes love possible. How irresistible would prove the instinct to diminish the debilitating rawness we feel in the roller-coaster of relationships? How tempting would it be to harden our hearts?

OBJECTION: THE UBIQUITY OF ENHANCEMENT?

These three radical enhancements which transhumanists propose fail, then, to revere human nature. Conversely put, revering human nature means refusing some of the most radical enhancements proposed by transhumanists.

The objection my argument immediately runs into is this: 'Don't we enhance all the time? Don't we already fail to revere human nature? So aren't transhumanist enhancements simply more of the same?'

Imagine I am holding this pen with my prosthetic arm. I am wearing glasses to see if what I have said is any good. I have cochlear implants to hear my mood music, Prozac to stave off paralysing depression, Ritalin to improve my concentration. More generally, I have a hip replacement. I've had a pacemaker fitted. I've been vaccinated against malaria.

Some of these alterations to my natural state are genuine. I have not, that is, left myself *au naturel*. I have intervened, taken myself in hand, improved myself. So how can these alterations not be classed as a series of enhancements?

The response to this objection hinges on a distinction between therapy and *genuine* enhancement. On this distinction, the improvements enumerated above can be described as treatments rather than enhancements insofar as they restore health. They restore functioning, reverse impairment, cure maladies. They put you back together. They make you better.

Transhumanists sometimes concede this. But there are other improvements, they insist, which certainly do go beyond therapy, which indeed enhance rather than restore. (And, therefore, because we already accept these improvements, we have no reason to reject others.)

Take education. We do not leave human beings 'as found'. To raise a child is to take responsibility for their enculturation: to impart knowledge and share language and pass on the ways of life. Are we to deny that education is fundamentally transformative, that it involves profoundly changing a human being, that it indeed constitutes an enhancement?

I think, however, that it's a mistake to view education as an enhancement. Why? It is here that the parallel with cultivation is critical. We said earlier that not every intervention in nature constitutes an encroachment for the reason that there are actions which accord with the intrinsic potential of the earth. 'Development' can be understood as a 'drawing out'. Similarly, education entails realizing the potentialities of a human being. It presupposes in the child a capacity that is receptive to being developed.

Consider an appalling case. A small child is kidnapped and sold to the circus. There she is kept in a cage and raised along with the animals. Never spoken to, she never develops her intrinsic capacity for language. Say that child was finally liberated and began to be nurtured. In one way, the grievous condition in which the child is found we could call natural, if we meant 'untouched'. But when we started to nurture her, we wouldn't say that that process was an enhancement, would we? We would be making up for something that should have happened as part of her normal life-cycle. We would be, though arriving late in the game, helping her to unfold in the way human beings tend to do.

In the end, then, transhumanists cannot sustain the objection that we enhance all the time (and therefore should embrace their proposals as but more of the same). What transhumanists propose are radically different changes to the human constitution.

NOTHING IS WRITTEN

Just because some people are temperamentally pessimistic doesn't mean disaster is unthinkable. There may be prophets of doom whom nobody likes very much, but even Cassandra was right in the end. Troy fell.

Aldous Huxley wrote *Brave New World* in 1931. Introducing the vat of embryos at the beginning of that notorious novel, Mr Forster rejoices that we have been brought at last 'out of the realm of mere slavish imitation of nature into the much more interesting world of human invention'. People have been invoking Huxley at every new juncture. Following the development of recombinant DNA in the 1970s, gene therapy again became a preoccupation of science fiction writers. John Varley's *The Ophiuchi Hotline* (1977) depicts intervention in the human genome to improve the human condition. By the mid-1980s gene technologies cropped up in books such as Greg Bear's *Blood Music* (1985) and Octavia E. Butler's *Xenogenesis* trilogy (1987, 1988, 1989). By the 1990s designer babies had become a literary staple, best tackled in the film *Gattaca* (1997), which depicts a world in which parents are encouraged to determine the genetic make-up of their offspring before birth. The fear of positive selection of specific traits, of the creation of designer babies, raised in each of these works has so far proved unfounded.

None of this means that the technological break-throughs of our moment won't lead to transhumanist attempts to reinvent the human. The grounds for this fear hark back to one of the key dynamics to emerge from the Baconian project – what has been called 'the technological imperative'. Accruing a track record of successfully holding sway over nature, harnessing natural power to their purposes, human beings understandably get the bug for it. Implicit in the mastery-of-nature picture is the assumption that because something is possible it is necessary. Something you now *know* you can do you *must* do. There is a presumption in favour of acting. The overcoming of one natural impediment only serves to bring others into view, to create new tasks to be tackled. Old impossibilities become new challenges, with the only thing holding us back being 'the present state of the science'.

In a telling aside, one pioneer of deep learning, Google's Geoffrey Hinton, has admitted that political regimes are likely to use AI to terrorize people. Asked why, given this prediction, he is still devoted to the development of AI, he said: 'The truth is that the prospect of discovery is too sweet.' In saying that, consciously or not he echoed Oppenheimer's famous comment on the atomic bomb: 'When you see something that is technically sweet, you go ahead and do it, and you argue about what to do about it only after you have had your technical success.'[24]

Similarly, in *A Crack in Creation*, their book about her discovery of CRISPR-Cas9, Jennifer Doudna and Samuel H. Sternberg discuss in detail the threats of the technology. They are circumspect. Not for them the headlong rush into reckless intervention in the germ-line. Caution, delay, democratic deliberation: all these they call for. Yet, after enumerating the risks, and calling for a moratorium, Doudna and Sternberg write this: 'Once a game-changing technology is unleashed on the world, it is impossible to contain it.' In other words, the technology's application is inevitable; it is an unstoppable force; nothing can hold it back. They continue: 'There's simply no way to unlearn this new knowledge, so we must embrace it.'[25]

The technological imperative thus grounds fears that the worst science fiction nightmares might be realized. Is that all that is to be said then? Is that the end of it? Must we conclude on a note of despair? To answer affirmatively would be to forget that the technological imperative is in fact a social construct. Hazardous technological developments occur because people such as the authors above acquiesce in the belief that they can't be stopped. History is littered with self-fulfilling prophecies, when the truth is that just as we are free to immolate ourselves (so we should not sit back and complacently dismiss dystopian scenarios), we are also free to resist, free to refuse the logics unleashed by certain technologies. For it is determinism that is the dream. Nothing is written.

The future has a past. A hundred years ago there was another movement which saw itself on the frontier of science, which stood for rationality and modernity and enlightenment and progress, and which constituted 'the conventional wisdom of the developed world'.[26] There was another elite movement that believed in the betterment of humanity. It had an agenda to which the leading institutions and politicians enthusiastically subscribed – Winston Churchill, then home secretary, William Beveridge, founder of the welfare state, public philosophers such as Bertrand Russell, luminaries in the established church. And it was Darwin's half-cousin Francis Galton who gave a name to it – 'eugenics'.

Immersed in statistical research, riveted by evolutionary biology and intuiting that genius was hereditary, Galton believed that a race of the gifted could be generated 'as surely as we can propagate idiots by mating cretins'. How was the improvement of the gene pool to be achieved? First by means of prevention – eliminating the unfit or discontinuing their lineages by way of sterilization. Second, by promotion – actively encouraging the propagation of better babies. Thus was born in Britain an agenda realized in Germany – the hundreds of thousands of compulsory sterilizations, the involuntary euthanasia of mental defectives and 'living burdens' as well as medals for particularly fecund mothers.

Transhumanists argue that none of what is happening today or planned for tomorrow constitutes eugenics. Why? Because, they insist, the routine abortion of newones identified as chromosomally compromised, or the selection of 'preferable' embryos through pre-implantation genetic diagnosis, or transhumanist dreams of genetic enhancement, is not mandated by the state but freely chosen by parents. Yet just because the route is different doesn't mean the destination is right. The world that would be created via 'liberal eugenics' – via, that is, the aggregation of individual choices rather than political coercion – is eerily similar.

But I mention this history to give reasons for hope. Mercifully, though after such atrocity, *that* eugenic future has finally been abandoned, thus demonstrating that there is no reason to assume that particular progressive scientific and technological projects are historical certainties. We can retreat from our advances. The cessation of the current public practice of (liberal) negative eugenics and the discarding of the dream of (liberal) positive eugenics are still possible. For again, nothing is written.

To conclude, if reverence is indeed the attitude that nature demands, if environmentalists are right – and I believe they are – to insist that the world is a gift that should invoke gratitude before all else, then it follows that we also face an imperative to revere human nature. That is what I have argued for in this chapter. The corollary is that, as we move into a century that will be replete with all manner of extraordinary technological possibilities, it is incumbent on us to reject attempts to master human nature by way of enhancing human faculties beyond all recognition.

6

Personal Responsibility: Why the Right Should Release Ex-Offenders

The story starts with abuse and drugs. Maria started using drugs as a teenager to forget her life as a child – memories of which were dominated by a stepfather with heavy hands. To pay for her habit Maria started selling. Caught at 18 with one vial of crack cocaine, she received a six- to ten-year prison sentence. But being locked up proved liberating. She took the opportunity to change course. She kicked her habit, earned her high-school diploma and took every vocational course the prison offered.

Six years later Maria returned to the Bronx with mixed feelings. She couldn't wait to see her siblings. But she didn't know what she would do to support herself. And she was right to feel apprehensive. Every time it was the same answer: no prospective employer wanted someone who had done time. She decided to apply for college, only to find, when she was filling out the federal loan application forms, that as a felon she was ineligible for assistance. Next Maria applied for a housing voucher, her sister having tired of a parole officer's unannounced visits, only to find she didn't qualify for that either.

The defeats kept coming, giving Maria little opportunity to exercise personal responsibility. Soon she was swept back into her old life: old friends, old habits, old measures. Resorting to selling and using drugs again, she fell into the arms of another abuser. The story starts with abuse and drugs. The story ends with abuse and drugs.[1]

For conservatives, perhaps it's the most fundamental principle of all, a principle endlessly invoked in op-eds and campaign speeches and often shaping social policies. The appeal to it is ubiquitous, by the leaders and at grassroots level; it is a mantra, a shibboleth. What's more, it is no modern conservative appropriation, an ideological co-optation, the result of a linguistic raid. No, the principle is rooted in centuries of conservative thought. And, unlike the Sanctity of Life, this principle plays on both sides of the Atlantic. It is the principle of *personal responsibility*.

But what does it mean, this peculiar phrase which manages to be 'at once anodyne and foreboding?'[2] It has to do with holding individuals to account for their actions. It has to do with setting out the necessary condition for social order. Thus former Prime Minister David Cameron argued: 'Many of today's issues come down to questions of responsibility. In the past, politicians have shied away from these questions, for fear of seeming judgemental. But we're never going to create a stronger, fairer society unless we address them.'[3] And thus we have the title of the reform Republicans secured from

President Clinton in 1996: the 'Personal Responsibility and Work Opportunity Reconciliation Act'.

We saw in earlier chapters how incendiary are the Right's foundational principles. To adhere to the Sanctity of Life is to set oneself up against second-wave feminism. To espouse family values, to defend marriage as the context where children have the best chance of flourishing, is to risk angering single parents. Well, President Reagan did not endear himself to the Left when, on entering office, he supplied this justification for punishment: 'We must reject the idea that every time a law's broken, society is guilty rather than the lawbreaker. It is time to restore the American precept that each individual is accountable for his own actions.'[4] Does not so forthright a pronouncement betray an inexcusable obliviousness to – or, worse, a cruelly deliberate ignoring of – the radically divergent social contexts in which individuals operate? How could he be so blind to the world? So insensitive to a person's background? So willing to offer a blanket condemnation that fails to discriminate between complex cases? Thus to affirm the principle of personal responsibility, the 'precept that each individual is accountable for his actions', is for many philosophically, politically and morally unacceptable. And it is precisely what I intend to do in this chapter.

Yet no sooner does one mount a defence of personal responsibility than one is confronted by questions of its consistent application. Taking criminal justice as my focus, I ask in this chapter what we would expect a system that honours personal responsibility to look like. Clearly, we would be unsurprised to find a retributive purpose of punishment alive and well; but what does a regime in which the 'collateral consequences' of punishment are so severe – the obstacles placed in Maria's way so many – say about our general approach to personal responsibility?

VITAL NEEDS OF THE HUMAN SOUL

'She didn't let her past define her.' 'He didn't blame his background.' 'She turned her life around.' 'He made something of himself.' We like to lionize those who have not allowed themselves to be shaped by the circumstances in which they were brought up, who refuse to believe that where they have come from will determine where they go, who have insisted they will not be the product of their environment but that their environment, in some sense, will be a product of themselves.

Our admiration in these cases, whether we admit it or not, bespeaks a deep-seated belief in the possibility of taking personal responsibility. Their stories are told – *they* tell their stories – as sources of inspiration to those who hail from the same kind of homes.

The philosopher Simone Weil, in her important book *The Need for Roots*, wrote this: 'Initiative and responsibility, to feel one is useful and even indispensable, are vital needs of the human soul.'[5] To dismiss personal responsibility is to dismiss the possibility of agency. How do we find ourselves in the world? Incapacitated, certainly – finite and vulnerable creatures, unable to fulfil all our desires, to realize all our dreams, frustrated in our attempts to fly. Yet to be in the world authentically is to take ownership of what remains near-to-hand to do, to make something of the opportunities we *are* afforded. We have the capacity and desire to act, and those possibilities are not always effaced by the limitations of our situation. We are pulled this way and that by our inclinations; we are pushed this way and that by other people; and yet to arrive at maturity is to achieve a certain self-consciousness, to experience a moment of 'reclaiming', to come to the realization that 'I too have a life to live'.[6]

Extending this thought, the philosopher T. M. Scanlon observes, 'it is often a good thing for a person to have what will happen to them depend on how he or she responds when presented with the alternatives under the right conditions.'[7] We are right to want our lives to reflect our choices. And we want this to be our manner of appearing in the world; we want, and rightly so, to be seen to have lives that reflect our choices: to be seen, that is, as agents.

This picture of agency is critically important, rooted, as it is, in the intuition that we thrive when we take charge of our lives, when we take responsibility for ourselves, when we hold ourselves accountable.

The problem is that the way agency is sometimes defended gives the impression that our most important responsibilities are all voluntarily assumed. Assuming responsibility is pictured like taking up a hobby. There is no obligation to take up marathon-running; but, once you have, it is important you live up to that commitment. This conception of agency certainly recognizes the need to be able to talk about people living up to their responsibilities but, crucially, the responsibilities are typically ones that have been at some point chosen. The contractual or 'voluntarist' paradigm is regnant here. Obligations are only obligations if *you* have been the one who has chosen to carry them out.

But what about those obligations we never assumed? Are not many of the most important responsibilities we face ones we never, or never fully, signed up to? I didn't pick my parents. What if my father dies and my mother happens to be radically incapacitated by a stroke when she is in her early fifties and I am in my early twenties? What is it incumbent on me to do in those circumstances? Financially? Emotionally? In terms of place: can I move away? Does that change my filial obligations?

Or what if I married young? 'We didn't know what we were doing.' It is often heard. 'We were nineteen.' 'We were in love.' 'I didn't know she would change so much.' Didn't know, that is, the sort of person she would grow up to be, or not to be; didn't know the sort of person I would grow up to be, or not to be. Didn't know how radically incompatible we would become. What does it mean to speak of fidelity in this case? Did my partial knowledge back then (when I entered into a marriage contract) abrogate my responsibility right now?

Or what if my partner and I decide we want children? We have saved for it. We think we are in the right place to provide a loving home. We have a realistic anticipation of what such an undertaking will entail. But then we discover the child has Down's syndrome, that she will have to live with us her whole life. We didn't sign up for *that*. Does that change our parental obligations?

The truth is, we awake to a world in which we are already immersed in demands. It is our 'native element'.[8] The force of those obligations does not track our strength of will as if the most binding obligations were the ones we assumed most freely. The upshot of this is that exercising personal responsibility is not wholly dependent on situation – whether we have signed up to our obligations or whether they happen to seem overwhelming ones.

THE QUANTUM MOMENT

Initiative and responsibility are vital needs of the human soul, and much of the time those needs can indeed be satisfied. We each have our own life to lead, and it is given to us to take the initiative. Yet, just as we must speak of the desirability and possibility of taking personal responsibility, of making something of our lives, so we must speak too of our failures to do this. And when it comes to speaking of these failures, we are not permitted to lose the very concept we have fought to rehabilitate: this notion of agency. If someone is going to praise me for summoning my powers to act, to execute a project, I must be prepared by the same token to have my failure spoken of as something that 'belongs to me'. Thus, the concept of guilt is dragged into view not as a mere social construct, an externally imposed norm that we reify, but as the corollary of our meaningful talk of agency.

This dynamic is very clear when it comes to the way we think about addiction; owning one's failures is a foundation stone in many treatment programmes.

Yet addiction talk doesn't leave things there, with the invocation to take responsibility in this retrospective sense. Ownership of failure is not the last step in the process. Consider this paragraph from a *Psychology Today* columnist:

The choice 'not to be that person any more' is at the core of self-responsibility. It is the quantum moment when a person re-defines themselves on their own terms and does so by taking hold of both their life and their personal experience of the world.[9]

Take, for example, the testimony of a recent graduate of the Process Recovery Center in New Hampshire. Shelley, 62, speaks of the way drinking had devastated her everyday life. 'Let's face it, when you're an addict, you're not thinking about buying food. You're thinking about the next drink.' In treatment, however,

> I learned how to become more responsible for myself and my sobriety ... The Process gave me opportunities. It's up to you to take advantage ... The Process got me back on 'life track'. Today, I am able to manage my sobriety. No one else is going to do it for me.[10]

The language of recovery assumes that agency is not like virginity: once lost, gone for ever. On the contrary, embedded in the notion of recovery is the possibility of *re*-assuming personal responsibility. Just as the notion of agency defies the determinism that would say you are but the product of your environment, so it defies the determinism that would say you are but the product of your failures.

All of this is to say that conservatives are right to insist on the principle of responsibility. For to lose that concept and instead assign all blame for wrongdoing on 'the system' would entrench states of disempowerment;

it would hold the person in contempt, would detract from their dignity. If we allow the precept of individual accountability to be shredded by a tornado of philosophical scepticism, we are shunning the possibility of being in the world in a certain way, in a way proper to our humanity, as those taking ownership of projects.

We are now in a position to arrive at our central question: the whereabouts of the principle of personal responsibility when it comes to our criminal justice systems. Retributivists might insist that personal responsibility is alive and well in the criminal justice system. Yet a picture of punishment according to which a person pays back a debt to society must have a notion of satisfaction. When in an individual's case are we permitted to speak of repayment? If a retributivist is required in this way to speak of the sufficiency of time served, this leads us to consider the *collateral consequences of crime.*

CIVIL DEATH

You confront it on the first form. Right there, unmissable, slapped right on the front.

> Have You or Any Person Who Will be Occupying the Apt. Ever Been Convicted, Charged, Arrested, Indicted, Pled Guilty or No Contest, or Received Deferred Adjudication or Probation to (a) Any Felony? Or (b) Any Misdemeanour Involving a Sexual Offense, Stalking, Illegal Use or Possession of Weapons, Assault, Battery, Theft, Fraud, Bad Checks, Criminal Damage to Property, Trespass, Vandalism, Illegal Possession or Sale of Drugs?[11]

This is the question posed to prospective tenants on the standard Georgia Apartment Association application for occupancy. Note that it makes no difference whether you have served your time and are no longer on probation. It makes no difference if your crime was entirely unrelated to the ban. (It is not just former vandals who might trash another house who are being excluded.) It makes no difference if you no longer pose a risk to society. Because you have been locked up now you are locked out. Once you have committed a crime you have become a criminal; an act has come to define your person; you are deemed the kind of person likely to commit more crime.

As many have observed, such a regime constitutes the resurrection of the historic pathology of 'civil death'.

It hurt pretty bad, *civiliter mortuus*. Technically, you were still alive, but in the eyes of the world you were dead. Your conviction left you in a state of 'civil death' – bereft of all rights, stripped of all protection. You were left radically exposed, in constant danger. In the Holy Roman Empire, someone declared civilly dead was known as *vogelfrei* ('free as a bird') – a sick joke. Now you were fair game, free to be killed with impunity.

Civil death was not confined to Europe. American legislatures too denied convicts the right to enter into contract, nullified marriages and barred entry to many professions.[12] As Supreme Court Justice Clark wrote in *Chaunt v. United States*, civil death results from an unwritten assumption that when the state sentences someone, it is able to extend 'limitations' or add 'disabilities'.

The law regards you as having a 'shattered character.' Therefore, in addition to any incarceration or fine, you are subject to legal restrictions and limitations on your civil rights, conduct, employment, residence and relationships. For the rest of your life, the United States and any State or locality where you travel or reside may impose at any time, additional restrictions and limitations they deem warranted. Their power to do so is limited only by their reasonable discretion.[13]

By the mid-twentieth century mainstream legal opinion had come to acknowledge the contradiction between the existence of significant collateral consequences and a commitment to punishment as proportional. The 1956 National Conference on Parole named the loss of civil rights 'an archaic holdover from early times' which needed to be abolished. And the 1960s and 1970s duly saw a decline in the number of state laws imposing collateral sanctions and an increase in the number of laws obliging automatic restoration of a convict's civil rights.[14]

What we face now then is a reversion. For while the extraordinary figures about incarceration may, finally, be getting more attention – the 2 million men and women behind bars in the US:[15] 25 per cent of the world's prisoners locked up in a country with close to 5 per cent of the world's population[16] – less well known are the roughly 65 million people with criminal records forced to live in a state of internal exile.[17]

We are also, finally, beginning to compute the significance of the radically disproportionate number of African-Americans and Hispanics imprisoned in America. But what of their fate upon release? As legal historian Michelle Alexander writes: 'Today a criminal freed from prison has scarcely more rights, and arguably less respect, than a freed slave or a black person living "free" in Mississippi at the height of Jim Crow.'[18] She continues:

> The 'whites only' signs may be gone, but new signs have gone up – notices placed in job applications, rental agreements, loan applications, forms for welfare benefits, school applications, and petitions for licenses, informing the general public that 'felons' are not wanted here. A criminal record authorizes precisely the forms of discrimination we supposedly left behind – discrimination in employment, housing, education, public benefits, and jury service. Those labelled criminals can even be denied the right to vote.

The confluence of race and civil death, the coincidence of the targeting of blacks and Hispanics and the exclusion that follows conviction have come to create a system that eerily resembles apartheid.

Take the fate of Michael Diaz-Rivera. A month away from starting university, while driving around Colorado Springs he was stopped and searched on the grounds of allegedly neglecting to signal when turning left. The seven grams of marijuana found on him proved sufficient to establish an intention to distribute, which he denied. On the advice of his public defender, he pleaded guilty to a Class 5 felony. 'I wasn't smart,' he says; 'I just didn't know about the legal system. In hindsight, I definitely should have fought it.' The time he served was not the problem – four months in a work-release programme and three years of probation. It was the collateral consequences that proved devastating. Speaking of the process of applying for a job or a flat, Diaz-Rivera says, 'before I can even talk about who I am to the community, the work I have done to overcome my past mistake, people are already looking at me as a felon. If I was able to get rid of that, I could let my true quality show.'[19]

Or take the testimony of a former prisoner to Washington DC's Neighborhood Legal Services Program: 'When you come home you aren't an asset to your family, you are a liability ... Food costs increase, housing, your kids, clothes. Odds are if you don't find a job, you'll go back to doing what you know. It's easier to get a gun and drugs than a job.'[20]

There are certainly some within the system who are now outraged. In a dramatic recent decision, Senior District Judge Frederick Bloch refused to imprison a woman who tried to smuggle 602 grams of cocaine into the US from Jamaica. Why? It was not that he doubted she had committed the crime, nor that it was not serious ('her criminal conduct is inexcusable'). Nor did he think he was showing mercy. No, his reasoning was that the sum of collateral consequences she was to face was so great that any punishment on top of that would be excessive. 'Remarkably,' he wrote in his opinion, 'there are nationwide nearly 50,000 federal and state statutes and regulations that impose penalties, disabilities, or disadvantages on convicted felons.'[21] He took the opportunity to launch an invective against a system in which 'district courts have no discretion to decide whether many of the collateral consequences should apply to particular offenders'.

The defence of this regime, or the reluctance to question it, is of course rooted in concerns about public safety. Society must be protected against future crime, and therefore against former criminals. The irony, however, in Britain as well as America, is that the recidivism rate – ex-offenders doing exactly what we are trying to stop them doing – is eye-wateringly high in part because of the cumulative effect of societal and state sanctions. As legal scholars Zachary Hoskins and Nora Wikoff write in 'Hard Times after Hard Time': 'When we consider the obstacles our society puts in the path of former prisoners trying to rebuild their lives, maybe we shouldn't be surprised by how many wind up committing crimes again in fairly short order.'[22]

So, the collateral consequences of crime are a form of punishment. Which returns us to our central question: what is the fate of the principle of personal responsibility in the criminal justice system?

When I was talking about addiction, I contended that enfolded in the principle of personal responsibility is the possibility of re-taking responsibility, the possibility that your past failures need not determine the rest of your life. If this is indeed correct, what we can then see is that the principle of personal responsibility is being ignored in a system that allows the collateral consequences of crime to be so devastating. We have created a world where reassuming responsibility is profoundly difficult.

WITH A LITTLE HELP FROM MY FRIENDS

I began this chapter defending the notion of personal responsibility as 'ownership of oneself'. To assume responsibility is to take oneself in hand, to realize the opportunities for action that the world *does* afford.

Now, in one sense there is something ineliminably individualistic about this, about saying that awakening to responsibility is awakening to a realization that 'I too have a life to live'. As Scanlon said, it is important that I am involved in the process of what happens to me, that I realize my own good rather than have a life, however rich, handed on a plate to me.

Yet just because taking responsibility is individualistic in this sense does not mean it is a principle that necessarily promotes individual*ism*. The mistake has been to conflate personal responsibility with *self-reliance*. What is the difference between these two senses of individualism? It has to do with the relation of the self to others.

Once upon a time humanity unshackled itself from the oppressive control of religion and tradition and began to think for itself. We call this great leap forward in the evolution of the species 'The Enlightenment'.

It's a foundational myth and, judging by recent titles (*Enlightenment Now*, Allen Lane, 2017), it is as bewitching as ever. Part of the reason it has proved so powerful is that it was self-propagated. The *philosophes* of the seventeenth and eighteenth century knew what they were up to. In his 'In Answer to the Question, "What is Enlightenment?"' Immanuel Kant writes that enlightenment is 'man's emergence from his self-incurred immaturity'. And what had that immaturity consisted in? 'Lack of resolution and courage to use one's own understanding without the guidance of another.'

Without the guidance of another. Thus was born an ideal, the ideal of the autonomous self, the lone operator, the unassailable agent. You and I may have emerged from a situation of radical neediness, brought into and brought up in the world by other people, but maturity consists in liberation from this dependence. In Kant's view adulthood constitutes a clean break with the circumstances of our unfolding.

One of the most famous intellectual treatises of the eighteenth century was a manual for education – Rousseau's *Émile*. For Rousseau, the making of a man involves his casting off both 'dependence on things, which is the work of nature, and dependence on people, which is the work of society'. Rousseau is adamant: 'each of us, unable to dispense with the help of others, becomes so far weak and wretched.' The authentic human life – what it means to flourish – is, in this view, to become self-sufficient.

We have every reason to question this asocial vision. The operation of agency, *my* involvement in *my* fate, hinges on the application of the form of intelligence we described in the last chapter as deliberative – 'the ability to weigh up options, to discriminate, to judge, to step back from our desires, to select our priorities, to discern our vocations, to think what we are doing'. Yet though it is what *I* have to do that is in question, my doing it well or badly so often varies according to how open I am to the input of other people. Do we not need critical friends, those who care about our good, to prevent our thinking becoming dysfunctional, to rescue us from fantasy and self-delusion, from becoming victims of our hopes and fears?[23] I need others to become myself. It is in the context of care and community that I learn to choose, to align my conduct with the good, to evaluate my reasons for action. Assistance is the precondition for agency. I get by with a little help from my friends.

In the criminal justice system 'assistance' goes by the name of 'rehabilitation'. In the UK an Act of 1907 assigned to the National Probation Service a mission to 'advise, assist and befriend'.[24] The assumption the law thought to embed in the criminal justice system was that relationship is instrumental to reformation. Whether it be education, intended as it is to prepare prisoners for a different kind of life upon release, the direct offer of friendship through mentoring (having an 'outsider' come alongside you during a period of such intense disorientation) or the kind of counselling that enables offenders to question the hazardous assumptions with which they have lived, rehabilitation can prove transformative. In many circles rehabilitation is much maligned as a purpose of punishment, grounded in the suspicion that it is simply modern cover for the sinister historic project to 'cure souls'. But in truth, if the resumption of personal responsibility is rooted in assistance, any punishment not centred on rehabilitation ignores the principle of personal responsibility.

'I have the motivation to be in control of my own choices – for how I see my future and how I see my children's future.' Dennis's story is an inspiring example of the possibility of rehabilitation, how the resumption of agency hinges upon the offer of assistance. Dennis's life started to implode when a fight at a basketball game landed him with an assault charge. He dropped out of Virginia State University, took a job as a cleaner, was caught selling drugs and put on probation. Then, after his brother was shot and killed, a routine drug test proved positive and he was sent to Norfolk City Jail.

As his release approached, Dennis, then 23 and the father of three children under six, was apprehensive

about the life that awaited him. Looking back, he says:
'I would find myself thinking all the time about how
[my kids] depend on me ... That's what I mean when I
say I needed to feel ready ... ready to handle whatever
things are like when I got out.'

What got him ready, as Dennis sees it, was a rehabilitation programme operated by Norfolk's Up Center.
Mentoring and group parenting classes helped him
think through strategies to deal with complex family
dynamics, particularly how he would engage with his
children's different mothers.

And it didn't just prepare him for this. Upon release
Dennis was told that his five-year-old child Kalani, who
suffered from chromosome deletion syndrome and had
been living with her mother, now needed to leave her
mother's house and find a new home. Dennis writes,
'When Kalani came to live with me, I needed to use
all my skills and all my confidence', and he attributes
his ability to meet this challenge to the rehabilitation
course. 'It was absolutely the right thing for me at the
right time.'[25]

We know, then, that rehabilitation *is* possible. Yet
in the criminal justice system as currently configured
Dennis is an outlier rather than a representative.

For instead of mentors, prisoners get guards. And
instead of drug treatment there is drug addiction. Take
these in turn.

In the UK, the 2010 coalition government's cut
in the prison budget led to staffing cuts which have
in turn led to overcrowding. With ratios of guards
to prisoners so dangerously low, officers have had
to focus myopically on prison safety just to fend off
disaster, and this has come at the detriment of any other

duties. Keeping order in a charged prison atmosphere is the condition for the realization of any other aim. Rehabilitation presupposes peace. Yet what we have seen in the UK are *increases* in violent assaults, upon both prisoners and officers. This has meant that the considerable potential of officers to act as mentors, to assist prisoners in rebuilding their lives, has remained untapped.

Secondly, prisoners are often more likely to acquire drug habits than lose them. 'If he'd have had 1 per cent of the right help, he'd be here now,' says Ben, a prisoner in The Mount, Hertfordshire, of his late fellow offender Rob Morris. A cannabis and alcohol addiction had led Rob, aged 23, to assault a man leaving a supermarket who refused to give him money.

His mother, Alison, was initially supportive of the sentence, hoping for rehabilitation: 'As his family, we were relieved, thinking the prison system will sort this out now.' But in fact, incarceration saw Rob graduate onto the more toxic drug Spice, the prison having failed to prevent drones delivering the drug at night. The devastating consequences for Rob were not just the side-effects of the drug – among them, zombie-like trances and the exacerbation of his mental ill-health – but also debt, bullying, alleged sexual assault and being held hostage.

Six months after release Rob was found in his living accommodation unit having inhaled his own vomit after drinking. The coroner's report acknowledged that 'an opportunity for beneficial treatment that this period of detainment afforded was missed'. While his mother concludes bitterly: 'Rob was sent to prison because he had committed a crime ... [But] he was sent into a den of drug taking ... So what was the point of it all?'[26]

What is the upshot, in relation to my overall argument, of the widespread failure of rehabilitation? It is this: we saw that taking responsibility hinges on receiving assistance and that rehabilitation is a form of assistance. Therefore, insofar as the state fails to deliver rehabilitation it fails to value personal responsibility.

JUSTICE TRIUMPHS OVER MERCY

When it comes to the criminal justice reform, we like to employ the language of 'mercy'. Criminals, we plead, need to be spared the atrocious conditions of prison. What are we calling for when we speak of mercy? We are calling for someone to intervene to abrogate the law. We are calling for representatives of the state to assume divine powers. (In *The Merchant of Venice* Portia says of mercy that it is an attribute of God himself so that 'earthly power doth then show likest God/ When mercy seasons justice'.)

A presidential pardon is a case in point. A pardon grants full legal forgiveness for a crime. It cuts short a sentence that should be served – a sentence to which, if it were to continue to be served, no objection could be raised. Despite the political statements a president might be making via his use of his constitutional powers – of the insanity of the war on drugs, for instance – legally the president is not implying that the offender has served their time and therefore that further punishment would be disproportionate and thereby unjust. No, upon a pardon the offender is being released prematurely – before he or she has served their time. Thus mercy can be said to triumph over justice.

What we have had in view here is the opposite case. Legal scholars Zachary Hoskins and Nora Wikoff ask us to imagine a prison warden coming to you on the last day of your sentence and saying, 'Well, you've completed your prison sentence, but we're going to go ahead and keep you in here permanently.'[27] We would be outraged. Yet something akin to this is precisely what is happening in the regime of sanctions imposed by the state on ex-offenders. And, therefore, when we call for the mitigation of the collateral consequences of crime we are not asking for mercy. We are asking for justice.

Conclusion

Moral Imagination

Edmund Burke, the great eighteenth-century Irish statesman, didn't feel he was being heard. He was railing against British colonialism, specifically the operations of the East India Company, and no one was taking any notice.

The 'nabobs', the newly minted directors of the East India Company, had returned to England and were using their money successfully to insinuate themselves into high society. Burke paints a vivid picture of the scene. Of the 'nabobs' he writes:

Arrived in England, the destroyers of the nobility and gentry of a whole kingdom will find the best company in this nation, at a board of elegance and hospitality. Here, the [British] manufacturer and husbandman will bless the just and punctual hand that in India has torn the cloth from the loom, or wrested the scanty portion of rice and salt from the peasant of Bengal [...] They [the nabobs] marry into your families; they enter into your senate; they ease your estates by loans; they raise their value by demand; they cherish and protect your relations which lie heavy on your patronage.

The English, by welcoming the former plunderers into their homes, by marrying off their daughters to them and making use of their money, were in effect condoning what they had done – all of which involved putting the Indians out of sight and out of mind. Burke thus had his work cut out for him in highlighting the 'grievance' of the Indian government. As he acknowledges at the end of the passage:

> It is an arduous thing to plead against abuses of a power which originates from your own country, and affects those whom we are used to consider as strangers.

Burke tries to elicit here what I want to call the 'moral imagination' of his listeners. He tries to awaken a faculty he believes is dormant, rather than extinct, in his fellow countrymen. He is at once assailing his audience for lacking something but also implying that they can regain it if they so choose. (It may be 'an arduous task', but he wouldn't be undertaking it if he thought it was futile.) He is assailing the workings of an empire. And evidence of whether or not their moral imaginations have been awakened, or are in good working order, will be judged by whether or not they can see that the abuses 'originate in their own country'.[1]

In this book we have waded into troubled waters – considering some of the most vexed moral questions we face as individuals and as citizens: the sexualization of culture, the breakdown of the family, the insufficiency of wages, the prospect of assisted dying, the failure of the criminal justice system, the environmental crisis, the perils of enhancement, the morality of abortion and the threat of gun violence. I have proposed that our best chance of getting it right, of aligning our action with the good, depends on our ability to slough off our political identities and affirm certain fundamental principles across the political spectrum – inclusivity, family values, sufficiency, personal responsibility, reverence for nature and the sanctity of life. We have to wrest ourselves free of package deals in order to determine the right courses of action.

I have taken some of the most compelling principles found on the Left and the Right and suggested which positions follow from a consistent application of those principles. And now that we have those positions on the table, now they are lined up alongside each other, we can see that something else is required. The resolution of each controversy, I propose, requires the exercise of this faculty of moral imagination to which Burke appealed.

In his important essay on moral imagination, the literary critic David Bromwich writes: 'A critical feature of the moral imagination [...] is that justice to a stranger comes to seem a more profound work of conscience than justice to a friend, neighbour, or member of my own community.' He adds: 'The more unlikely or remote the path of sympathy, the surer the proof of moral imagination.'[2]

'Remote' is right. For what I want to say is that in societies as complex as ours fellow countrymen can be as much strangers as the Indians were to the British in the age of empire. The concerns of one group within a

171

complex society can be as remote to another as the fate of one country is to another.

THOSE WHOM WE ARE USED TO CONSIDER AS STRANGERS

When I was talking about guns, I alluded to the 'way of life' argument that many conservatives employ to oppose greater restrictions. Why should law-abiding Americans who live in the rural areas have their freedom to bear arms curtailed in cities they'll never visit, or in states that might as well be different countries? The chief executive of the National Shooting Sports Foundation wrote recently:

> If you are in a city environment, where all you see are the anti-personal uses of firearms, you think guns are anti-personal; if you grow up in rural areas where guns are accepted, are part of life, used for recreation, sports, family gatherings [...] you see that there is nothing wrong [with owning them].[3]

His assumption is that one's immediate situation has to determine the horizon of concern. If you live in the city, you will identify with one group; if in the country, another. This demonstrates why the transformation of gun culture in America hinges on the exercise of moral imagination – the determination to see what typically remains hidden from view.

In his passionate appeal, Burke was not presenting the Indians as a charity case. No, India was part of the British empire, which meant that Burke addressed people who were in various ways implicated in the operations of the nabobs. It was incumbent on the British to act on Burke's report of the injustices perpetrated in their name. Ignoring his call would constitute negligence. By accepting the nabobs back with open arms, British high society was failing to exercise its moral imagination, something for which it was directly culpable.

Similarly, just as the Indians belonged to the same empire as the British, so rural conservatives dismissive of gun control belong to the same country as kids caught in the crossfire in Chicago. And it takes moral imagination to see that.

The same holds true in the case of assisted suicide, which we explored in Chapter 1. Consider philosopher John Arras's reflection on the unintended consequences of legalizing assisted dying. I think it a fine and important example of the exercise of the moral imagination.

> These victims of the current policy [prohibiting assisted dying] are easy to identify: They are on the news, the talk shows, the documentaries [...] The victims of legalization, by contrast, will be largely hidden from view; they will include the clinically depressed eighty-year-old man who could have lived another year of good quality if only he had been adequately treated, and the fifty-year-old woman who asks for death because doctors in her financially stretched [insurance company] cannot, or will not effectively treat, that mysterious pelvic pain [...] these victims will not get their pictures in the papers, but they all will have faces and they will all be cheated of good months or perhaps even years.[4]

The commitment to inclusivity, I argued, constitutes one of the Left's most compelling principles. It is a principle that required moral imagination in the early twentieth century, for holders of power to bring into view the marginalized elderly. And it is a principle, as Arras indicates, that requires moral imagination today. Such an exercise is required for exactly the same reason in the Burkean case and the case of gun control – older people who might be affected by the introduction and normalization of assisted dying may be unseen by us but, given the political reality, belong to us.

'Who might be affected.' Is this not pure speculation? Mere conjecture? Unfounded prediction? Perhaps it is too tenuous to act on behalf of imagined groups, to weigh our decisions against potential constituencies who could be harmed (older people who could feel pressured to commit suicide). How are we to justify this use of the moral imagination?

The answer is that moral imagination is a form of prudence, and prudence is future-oriented. When diplomats and statesmen reach a just settlement to end a war, they are not just trying to respond fairly to what has been – to issue a retrospective judgement – but are also looking to a state of affairs that will prove workable in future. They are thinking of generations to come. Similarly, we don't refuse to consider the consequences of our actions because those affected are not near at hand. To be engaged in the special work of moral imagination is to throw yourself into the future and consider carefully the unintended side-effects and easily ignored impacts on those to come. Moral imagination looks forward and not just sideways. We do not just look around; we look ahead. We do not just see what is but imagine what will be.

Imagining what will be is even more demanding in the case we examined in Chapter 5 – transhumanism. Again, what does it mean to act on behalf of those who are hidden from view? Burke again is incisive: 'Society', he insisted, is 'a partnership not only between those who are living, but between those who are living, those who are dead, and those who are to be born.' The moral imagination extends from those remote to us in space to those remote to us in time.

It is argued that there can be no rational objection to positive eugenics – to selection of embryos on the basis of IQ or genetic engineering itself – because no one can be said to be harmed. For if the child had not been created that way she would not exist, and therefore, unless she deems her life not worth living at all, she cannot turn around to her parents and complain they have wronged her by, for instance, upsetting the balance of her mind (the detrimental consequence of cognitive enhancement that we predicted).

But here is where the moral imagination comes in. It is fiendishly difficult to answer this philosophical conundrum – the so-called 'non-identity' problem. Yet just as we rightly take into account future generations when we consider our treatment of the environment, so we are also obliged to consider the impact that the realization of transhumanist goals would have on our descendants.

On some occasions the awakening of moral imagination is a result of the strident advocacy of people such as

Edmund Burke. Men and women act on their privileged access to the predicament of a people and then render it visible. It is incumbent on us to see what has been shown, not to turn away our faces; not avert our eyes. But that is not the only model of how the moral imagination is exercised. Sometimes what is required is not only a passive response, but active exposure.

At an early point in Shakespeare's great play, King Lear waves away the reality of poverty with the famous exclamation

> O reason not the need! Our basest beggars
> Are in the poorest things superfluous.

Even the very poorest, he declares, have more than they need (thus justifying the refusal of alms). Now Lear, it quickly becomes apparent, can only believe this of the poor because he hasn't *seen* them. They remain only notional subjects. Later in the play, after his downfall renders him destitute, Lear encounters the basest beggars for himself and is moved to this exclamation:

> Poor naked wretches, wheresoe'er you are,
> That bide the pelting of this pitiless storm,
> How shall your houseless heads and unfed sides,
> Your loop'd and window'd raggedness, defend you
> From seasons such as these?

The authenticity of Lear's pity is then demonstrated by his immediate assumption of responsibility: 'O, I have taken too little care of this!' Earlier he issues the all-important injunction to anyone who has means:

Expose thyself to feel what wretches feel,
That thou mayst shake the superflux to them,
And show the heavens more just.

A willingness to shake 'the superflux' – that is, for those with means to give the *excess* of their resources – is evidence that the moral imagination is being exercised.

All too often one hears those on the Right insisting that the working poor have never had it so good. Do they need more resources? We hear them say, in effect, 'Reason not the need!' But any reckoning with the realities of working poverty, the realities we examined in Chapter 2, reveals many men and women not to be 'in the poorest things superfluous'. Family life is under fire. The problem is that the ways in which employers have historically been exposed to those realities – through unions, for instance – have been eviscerated. Mediating, representative institutions have been dismantled. And because labour has been distanced from capital, the exercise of moral imagination enjoins employers actively to expose themselves to the very different kind of life of those they employ.

It is the same when it comes to the criminal justice system. The whole point of prisons is to create distance between one sub-group and the rest of society.

'President Visits Prison.' Should that be a story? On 16 July 2015, President Obama visited the Federal Correctional Institution El Reno, 30 miles west of Oklahoma City. He passed through the gates and under the fences, peered into a nine-by-ten-foot cell and spoke to six inmates. The reason it was a story was because he was the first president to do so. All too often a political class has put out of sight and out of mind a group of people whose fates they determine. So too, then, does the reform of the criminal justice system hinge on exposure to 'those whom we are used to consider strangers'.

Finally, what of our remaining case – the phenomenon of sexual consumerism we explored in Chapter 3? Here also it is particularly taxing to bring into view those affected by our common culture. Moral imagination is arduous; it takes work – to see who is impacted by the culture we have shaped, the ways of life we have left unquestioned. We saw the Left's perspicacity when it comes to identifying children as the victims of a rampantly materialistic culture. It takes even more work to revisit our assumptions about our sexual culture – in particular, our deeply held belief that consent is the sufficient condition of rightly ordered relationships – and therefore to see we have endorsed a way of life not oriented to their good. It means being alert to the alterity of their experiences, and to a malaise we find at first unfathomable in our own terms.

MRS JELLYBY RIDES AGAIN?

So, without moral imagination we cannot act on the critical questions we have explored in this book. Yet in our cultural context there are profound obstacles to the exercise of the moral imagination. Here I want to explore three.

To get a grip on the first obstacle, we have to see how one way of thinking about moral imagination is as a form of *cosmopolitan sympathy*.

'Cosmopolitanism' as a term can be traced back to the Cynics, a philosophical school in the fourth century

BC. When Diogenes was asked where he came from, 'kosmou polites' was his reply (literally, 'citizen of the cosmos' – a polites was someone who belonged to the polis, but in this new case that polis was the kosmos). What exactly did it mean to be a citizen of the world? It meant that a person's duties were to the 'world', not connoting the earth itself (that is, reverence for nature) but rather everyone in it, the earth's inhabitants. The term was normative, action-guiding; referring to how things ought to be done. It suggested that the scope of someone's ethical concern should be as broadly construed as possible. The idea captured by the notion of 'cosmopolitanism' is that, as the philosopher Kwame Anthony Appiah puts it, 'we have obligations to others that stretch beyond those to whom we are related by the ties of kith and kind'.[5]

Developed by the Stoic schools of Greek and Roman philosophy,* cosmopolitanism surfaces dramatically among the earliest Christian writers in the first century AD. In a key text, St Paul writes: 'There is neither Jew nor Greek, there is neither bond nor free, there is neither male nor female; for ye are all one in Christ Jesus.'[6] This emphasis on the oneness of humanity and the equality of peoples generates the exhortation to lift up one's eyes from the concerns of one's immediate fellows and look to a wider ethical horizon. The Christian is called to love his neighbour. But who is his neighbour? That

---

* The Stoics considered the whole cosmos a polis because it was governed by divine law of which every man, because of the endowment of his reason, was cognizant. Philo, the philosopher of the first century AD, put it like this: 'A man who is obedient to the law, being, by so doing, a citizen of the world, arranges his actions with reference to the intention of nature, in harmony with which the whole universal world is regulated.'

category is radically expanded in Christian thought to include strangers as well as friends.

The cosmopolitan ideal was rooted for centuries in the concrete institutional form of one church stretched across huge swathes of the known world. But cosmopolitanism also survived Christendom, becoming a mainstay of Enlightenment thought. Thus Thomas Paine proclaimed: 'The world is my country; all mankind are my brethren, and to do good is my religion.' Or, more expansively, the German philosopher Christoph Martin Wieland captured its essence in 1788:

Cosmopolitans [...] regard all the peoples of the earth as so many branches of a single family, and the universe as a state, of which they, with innumerable other rational beings, are citizens, promoting together under the general laws of nature the perfection of the whole.[7]

With the Declaration of the Rights of Man in 1789 and Kant's proposed 'league of nations', it was the emancipation of the whole of humankind the Enlightenment thinkers set out to achieve.

The cosmopolitan creed is historic, then. But no less historic is the backlash against it. The idea of abjuring local allegiances, of transcending partialities, has long been the subject of derision – for the reason that it has been considered morally suspect.

What is that suspicion founded upon? The suspicion is that preoccupation with an abstract creed will function as an excuse for evading more immediate responsibilities. 'Friend of men, and enemy of almost every man he had to do with', Thomas Carlyle said of the Marquis de

Mirabeau, who wrote *L'Ami des hommes* but imprisoned his own son. Similarly, Burke complained of Rousseau (who deposited his five children in an orphanage): 'A lover of his kind, but a hater of his kindred.' The suspicion is that abstract love for general humanity will inevitably eclipse or replace concrete love for the person who lives next door.

In Charles Dickens's novel *Bleak House* that person is Joe, the crossing-sweeper. Joe sleeps every night on the doorstep of Mrs Jellyby's house – 'a telescopic philanthropist' who expends all her energy on overseas charitable projects while ignoring the plight of the boy at her door. Dickens's satire of this kind of cosmopolitanism (and that satire was influential enough to have a 'syndrome' named after Mrs Jellyby in moral philosophy) captures this dynamic at the heart of the critique of cosmopolitanism: the evasion of responsibility, the ignorance of special responsibilities, the neglect of the ties that bind. The suspicion is that opening your eyes to the wider world means shutting your eyes to what's in front of you.

'If you believe you are a citizen of the world, you are a citizen of nowhere', the British prime minister Theresa May declared, both responding to and in effect stoking a suspicion of cosmopolitan sympathy in our cultural moment. She was tapping into the feeling of many that cosmopolitan sympathy is merely the luxury of a liberal elite who, though they may be great global philanthropists, are unconcerned with the injustices on their doorsteps, of middle-class professionals who reside in international cities and give generously to overseas development projects while ignoring the devastation that drug addiction has wrought in the estates and projects opposite their own houses.

If moral imagination is to be understood, as it should be, as a form of cosmopolitan sympathy, then many might be unwilling to do what it takes to respond, in their moral choices, to 'those whom we are used to consider as strangers'.

The question to ask, however, is whether we in fact face a sharp binary choice? Are concern for the remote other and concern for the next-door neighbour mutually exclusive? Is sympathy a zero-sum game? Certainly, cosmopolitanism can serve as an excuse for neglect of our fellows. But does it have to? Edmund Burke also exhorted individuals to identify with their communities: 'To be attached to the subdivision, to love the little platoon we belong to in society, is the first principle (the germ as it were) of public affections.' But he doesn't leave it there. He continues: 'It [this love of the little platoon] is the first link in the series by which we proceed towards a love to our country, and to mankind.' Rather than cosmopolitanism, the exercise of moral imagination, being a substitute for loving our own communities, loving our own communities provides the foundation for the exercise of moral imagination. How? First, by providing an education in seeing, a sustained attention to the particularities of a predicament in which our neighbours find themselves. Secondly, by providing the training ground for the kind of self-sacrifice required as a response to a recognition of those predicaments.

WHERE THERE'S A WILL THERE'S NO WAY

Fear of bad faith might deter us from exercising our moral imagination. A second deterrent might be a fear that any effort we make will prove futile.

There are those who argue that, even if our cosmopolitan sympathies are evoked, the scale of the problems we face will inevitably prove overwhelming, that even where there's a will there's no way. Yuval Noah Harari contends that 'justice demands not just a set of abstract values, but also an understanding of cause-and-effect relations', and 'unfortunately, an inherent feature of our modern global world is that its causal relations are highly ramified and complex'.[8] The idea is that the world – and again I assume that what is said about our global context holds true for modern nation states – is simply too complicated for us to get a meaningful grip on the far-reaching consequences of our actions. And if we can't grasp the causal relations, we stand no chance of making the kind of profound changes that could transform the lives of those whom we are used to considering as strangers. Any attempt to exercise moral imagination will be frustrated.

The problem with this view is its underestimation of the power of social movements.

Certainly, insofar as these sweeping dismissals of the exercise of moral imagination have in mind public policy as the primary engine of social change, scepticism is warranted. All too often policy is a blunt tool. Political elites, genuinely captivated by a vision of change, try to pull the levers of power to achieve certain outcomes. But then epistemic limitations, the difficulty of gauging those cause-and-effect relations, lead to the unleashing of unintended side-effects. Or efforts fail because they establish incentives and disincentives that work on the erroneous assumption that citizens are always rational actors.

But what our current moment is confirming dramatically is that it is culture and not policy that is the primary engine of social change. And not just movements that rally or 'out' people secretly already sympathetic to a cause; social movements which change minds too.

Take #MeToo. It is one thing to say, 'Here is a practice from a certain time in history which, while everyone considered it wrong, was far more prevalent than people thought.' In that instance the revelation would be that more people were complicit than we thought – owing, perhaps, to lax law enforcement. Altogether different is the phenomenon of #MeToo. For what we are doing is looking back at past practices and realizing that what was considered innocuous behaviour is in fact sexual harassment. The sort of social change we are seeing at the moment is therefore all the more remarkable, and a source of even greater hope that the predicaments we have explored in this book can also change.

THEY ARE ALL OUR CHILDREN

The third and final obstacle to the exercise of moral imagination is the suspicion, emanating from evolutionary psychology, that acting on behalf of remote strangers somehow goes against our nature.

The story is told that a journalist in the Bosnian conflict of the early 1990s was crouching in an alleyway reporting on a street battle. Suddenly a young girl tried to run across the street and was hit by sniper fire. A man dashed out after her, picked her up and carried her to the alley where the journalist was taking cover. The man pleaded with the journalist, 'Please can you help? My child has been shot.' The journalist took the man and the child to his car a few blocks away and rushed them to hospital. The doctors did all they could to save her life, but it was too late. Once they had been informed, the man and the journalist retreated to the bathroom to wash the blood off their hands and clothes, whereupon the man turned to the journalist and said, 'We have to find her parents.' The journalist looked back perplexed. 'I thought you said she was your child.' The man just kept washing his hands. 'They are all our children,' he said.

Now read this, from sociobiologist Michael Ghiselin:

> The economy of nature is competitive from beginning to end. Understand that economy, and how it works, and the underlying reasons for social phenomena are manifest. They are the means by which one organism gains some advantage to the detriment of another. No hint of genuine charity ameliorates our vision of society, once sentimentalism has been laid aside. What passes for co-operation turns out to be a mixture of opportunism and exploitation [...] Scratch an 'altruist' and watch a 'hypocrite' bleed.[9]

In Ghiselin's view, it is impossible to understand a story like this on its own terms. For if natural selection benefits selfish organisms, how we can we make sense of the villager's act of extravagant self-abnegation? More precisely, 'if natural selection favours traits that cause individuals to survive and reproduce better than other individuals, and if altruism increases the survival and reproduction of *others* at a cost to the altruist, then how can altruistic traits evolve?'[10]

In light of this dilemma, sociobiologists explain (away) acts such as the villager's as an evolutionary 'misfiring'. Long ago on the savannah, they contend, we made sacrifices toward only close kin or 'potential reciprocators'. Now though, while our context is radically different, the rule of thumb, the altruistic instinct, persists – a useless, potentially dangerous (in terms of our fitness) evolutionary hangover. In any case, the villager is deceived as to what he thinks he is doing. He may *seem* to have no ulterior motive; he may, afterwards, have told himself that story. But in fact, he is acting from a fundamentally selfish instinct that might be out of date but which is still very much in place. On this account, 'altruism is in fact only selfishness deceived.'[11]

I introduce this case to demonstrate why contemporary evolutionary psychology struggles to make sense of the class of obligations we have before us, obligations to 'those whom we are not used to consider strangers'. Evolutionary psychology struggles to make sense of moral imagination. And as if the Bosnian case wasn't challenging enough to account for, the difficulty is compounded in the class of obligations we have in view. That is, for the Bosnian villager, the child was there in person. But in the cases we have in mind, the other remains remote, stays a stranger, and not one ever likely to become a friend. A gun owner in rural Appalachia may never meet the child caught in the crossfire in Chicago. (One sociobiologist tries to square this by explaining away our donations to victims of famine on the grounds that our discriminatory 'equipment' has been 'fooled' by the media into 'mistaking those victims for immediate neighbours' and thus operating from the instinct that we will get something back from them.)

In his influential book *The Righteous Mind: Why Good People Are Divided by Politics and Religion*, Jonathan Haidt writes:

It would be nice to believe that we humans were designed to love everyone unconditionally. Nice, but rather unlikely from an evolutionary perspective. Parochial love – love within groups – amplified by similarity, a sense of shared fate, and the suppression of free riders, may be the most we can accomplish.[12]

What we find in contemporary evolutionary psychology is constant slippage from description (accounts of how we humans were designed to live) to prescription (recommendations on what we ought morally to do now.) Haidt *is* in the business of offering advice, but his denial of this serves to mask the real dynamic going on, which is that the description determines and delimits the prescription. We can see that clearly here. Because we are like *this* (parochial in our affections), there's no point trying *that* ('to love everyone unconditionally').

Someone said that we are creatures who paint pictures of the world and then live by them. We are told that moral imagination is 'rather unlikely from an evolutionary perspective', and then, accordingly, we discourage ourselves from exercising it. Yet we are also free, and the time has come to deface the picture.

TO END, TO BEGIN

Answering many of the vexed questions of this book requires moral imagination. The older person who feels herself a burden, the underpaid worker, the prisoner, the teenager facing the reality of sexual consumerism, the child vulnerable to gun violence, our descendants – to many of us they are remote strangers. Only by considering them can we escape package-deals and escape ideology.

Yet at every turn we are told that any attempt to exercise our moral imagination is bound to fail. We are told that we aren't able to care about the remote stranger without neglecting the next-door neighbour. We are told that the world is just too complex for our actions to make any difference. We are told that we simply don't have it in us to be altruistic. Yet why must we underestimate ourselves so? Certainly, we are creatures capable of cruelty. But we are also remarkable: we are capable of love, full of potential. Certainly, we are shaped by our environments. But have we to be *determined* by them? Aren't we the creatures able to step back and question all that we are and all that we have been, and to act on that evaluation, transforming ourselves and our purposes? We live in a world, we are reminded *ad nauseam*, which is socially constructed. Doesn't that mean we can, by the same token, deconstruct and reconstruct it? We must begin by believing in ourselves again.

ACKNOWLEDGEMENTS

First and foremost, my immense gratitude goes to the Institute for Advanced Studies in Culture at the University of Virginia, which awarded me the Wolterstorff Postdoctoral Fellowship to write this book. I have been overwhelmed by the generosity shown to me there by director James Davison Hunter, Joe Davis, Josh Yates, Tony Lin, Jackson Lears and the staff, who have created a very special intellectual community. In terms of support, I also cannot sufficiently express my thanks to Paul and Sabina Marshall, Crispin and Nichola Odey, Ken and Fi Costa, John and Kara Kim, and our family away from home – Guy and Susie Speers. In terms of research, my thanks are due to Tatiana Lozano, Rick Yoder and Henry Gumbel for their meticulous work as well as to the many people who kindly granted me interviews, read drafts and indulged my often embarrassingly basic questions, among them Denis Alexander, Peter Saunders, Trevor Stammers, Willis Jenkins, Christopher Kaczor, Samuel Matlack, Christian Guy, Johann Neem, John Kim, Jonathan Aitken, Danny Kruger, John Wyatt and Matt Ridley.

My own family have been with me through thick and thin on this project – my parents, John and Eleanor, my parents-in-law, Andy and Judy, my children, Connie and Vera (born in Charlottesville while I was working on this book), my wonderful brother and sister-in-law, Marcus and Carey, and, above all, my extraordinary wife, Holly.

To Aristotle, or the school of Aristotle, is attributed the saying 'What we do through our friends we do, as it were, ourselves.' My thinking has been shaped by countless conversations with brilliant colleagues who have been so generous with their time: in Charlottesville – Rebecca Stangl, Charles Mathewes, Trenton Merricks, Nick Frank, Colin Bird, Greg Thomson and Matt Crawford; in London – Jonny Gumbel, James Orr, Jonathan Tepper, Freddie Sayers, Maurice Glasman and remotely – Tom Simpson, Charles Foster, Rich Nathan. I am also immensely grateful for my teachers Jacqueline Whitaker and Oliver O'Donovan; for their encouragement at key junctures in the writing process to Susan Arellano, Rowan Williams and Xandra Bingley; and for poring over drafts to Aaron Kheriaty, Frank Curry and Micah Lott – I have benefited so much from their philosophical acumen. I must thank Philippa Stroud and the Legatum Institute for their hospitality in the autumn of 2017. Finally, I am indebted to Jay Tolson, Talbot Brewer and Philip Lorish, without whose help I simply could not have written this book.

I dedicate this book to Patricia Park, my honorary grandmother, who was a brilliant woman, and a source of great inspiration and encouragement to me throughout my life. Before she died, she insisted I should not dedicate a book to her. She hasn't got her way on this one.

NOTES

Introduction: Package-Deal Ethics

1 Benedict Anderson, *Imagined Communities: Reflections on the Origin and Spread of Nationalism* ([1983] London: Verso, 2006), p. 6.
2 Quoted in Timothy J. Main, *The Rise of the Alt-Right* (Washington, DC: Brookings Institute, 2018), p. 5.
3 Quoted in ibid, p. 169.
4 Amy Chua, *Political Tribes: Group Instincts and the Fate of Nations* (London: Bloomsbury, 2018), p. 207.

1: Inclusivity: Should Liberals Back Assisted Suicide?

1 The anecdote is taken from Rachel Aviv's article, 'The death treatment', *The New Yorker*, 22 June 2015; https://www.newyorker.com/magazine/2015/06/22/the-death-treatment [accessed 28 February 2016].
2 Charles Booth, *Old Age Pensions and the Aged Poor: A Proposal* (London: Macmillan & Co., 1899), p. 15.
3 Quoted in David Hackett Fischer, *Growing Old in America* (New York: Oxford University Press, 1973), p. 158.
4 https://www.merriam-webster.com/dictionary/geriatric [accessed 30 April 2019].
5 Quoted in Joan Metge, *Rautahi: The Maoris of New Zealand* (Oxford: Routledge, 1967), p. 20.
6 National Resource Center for American Indian, Alaska Native, and Native Hawaiian Elders, 'Qualitative report conferences of Alaska native elders: our view of dignified aging'; https://arctichealth.org/media/pubs/85247/yr1_2qualitative.pdf [accessed 30 April 2019], p. 21.

7 Anthony Giddens, *The Transformation of Intimacy: Love, Sexuality and Eroticism in Modern Societies* (Cambridge: Polity Press, 1992), p. 98. Giddens is referring to the work of Janet Finch and Jennifer Mason.

8 Centre for Social Justice, 'Age of opportunity: transforming the lives of older people in poverty', June 2011; http://www.centreforsocialjustice.org.uk/core/wp-content/uploads/2016/08/20110629_AgeofOpportunity.pdf [accessed 30 April 2019].

9 CNN, 'The elder orphans of the baby boom genex'; http://www.cnn.com/2015/05/18/health/elder-orphans/ [accessed 24 June 2015].

10 Ibid.

11 Amy Ziettlow and Naomi Cahn, 'The honor commandment: law, religion and the challenge of elder care', *Journal of Law and Religion*, June 2015, pp. 1–31.

12 Joyce Varner, 'The elder orphans: who are they?', *The Alabama Nurse*, 32:3, September–November 2005, pp. 19–20.

13 Michael Banner, *The Ethics of Everyday Life: Moral Theology, Social Anthropology and the Imagination of the Human* (Oxford: Oxford University Press, 2014), p. 120.

14 Oregon Revised Statute, 127.805 s.2.01; 127.810 s.2.02. Form of the written request.

15 David Velleman, 'Against the right to die', in *Beyond Price: Essays on Life and Death* (Cambridge: Open Book Publishers, 2015), p. 13.

16 Ian M. Ball, Robert Sibbald, Robert D. Truog, *The New England Journal of Medicine*, 379:10, 6 September 2018.

17 I am indebted to Philip Lorish for this way of putting the point.

18 'The Right to Die', 27 July 2015; https://www.economist.com/leaders/2015/06/27/the-right-to-die [accessed 30 April 2019].

19 This account of Mr Conway's story, and all quotations, are taken from the Campaign from Dignity in Dying; https://features.dignityindying.org.uk/noel-conway/ [accessed 16 October 2018].

20   Gilbert Meilaender, 'I want to burden my loved ones', *First Things* (1991); https://www.firstthings.com/article/2010/03/i-want-to-burden-my-loved-ones [accessed 30 April 2019].

2: Family Values: Why Social Conservatives Should Raise Wages

1   Jordan G. Teicher, 'Fast food workers photograph what life is like when you make less than $15 an hour', *Slate*, 18 May 2015; https://slate.com/culture/2015/05/fast-food-workers-photograph-their-daily-lives-in-the-exhibit-i-too-am-america.html [accessed 17 February 2019].

2   Ibid.

3   Quoted in Robert Reich, *Saving Capitalism: For the Many, Not the Few* (London: Icon, 2017), pp. 136–7.

4   Melina Ryzik, '"I, Too, Am America" shares snapshots from workers living on the edge', *New York Times*, 1 May 2015; https://www.nytimes.com/2015/05/02/arts/design/i-too-am-america-shares-snapshots-from-workers-living-on-the-edge.html [accessed 17 February 2019].

5   The Conservative and Unionist Party, *Forward Together: Our Plan for a Stronger Britain and a Prosperous Future* (May 2017).

6   Quoted in Laurel Elder and Steven Greene, *Politics of Parenthood: Causes and Consequences of the Politicization and Polarization of the American Family* (New York: SUNY Press, 2012), p. 35.

7   'David Cameron: family values the key to a responsible society', *Daily Telegraph*, 29 March 2009; http://www.telegraph.co.uk/news/politics/5070968/David-Cameron-family-values-the-key-to-responsible-society.html [accessed 16 September 2017].

8   The Heritage Foundation, 'The true origin of society', 16 October 2013; http://www.heritage.org/political-process/report/the-true-origin-society-the-founders-the-family [accessed 16 September 2017].

9   Focus on the Family, 'Our mission', http://www. focusonthefamily.com/about/foundational-values [accessed 17 September 2017].

10   Andrew Cherlin, *The Marriage Go-Round: The State of Marriage and the Family in America Today* (New York: Vintage, 2009), p. 20.

11   Zadie Smith, *On Beauty* ([2005] London: Penguin, 2006), p. 398.

12   See Gingerbread, 'One in four: a profile of single parents in the UK', February 2018; https://www.gingerbread.org.uk/ wp-content/uploads/2018/02/One-in-four-a-profile-of-single-parents-in-the-UK.compressed.pdf [accessed 1 May 2019].

13   Jane Miller and Tess Ridge, 'Work and relationships over time in lone-mother families', Joseph Rowntree Association, July 2017.

14   Arthur Marwick, *The Sixties: Cultural Revolution in Britain, France, Italy, and the United States, c.1958– c.1974* (Oxford: Oxford University Press, 1998), p. 381.

15   Quoted in W. Bradford Wilcox, 'The evolution of divorce', *National Affairs*, Fall 2009, p. 83; https://www.nationalaffairs. com/publications/detail/the-evolution-of-divorce [accessed 25 February 2019].

16   Cherlin, *The Marriage Go-Round*, p. 32.

17   This is a figure for the US, given in Wilcox, 'The evolution of divorce'.

18   Ibid., p. 90.

19   Sendhil Mullainathan and Eldar Shafir, *Scarcity: The True Cost of Not Having Enough* (London: Penguin, 2013).

20   Ibid.

21   Kayla's story is trailed across Robert Putnam's *Our Kids: The American Dream in Crisis* (New York: Simon and Schuster, 2015).

22   Quoted in Jodi Kantor's report 'Working anything but 9 to 5', *New York Times*, 13 August 2014; https://www. nytimes.com/interactive/2014/08/13/us/starbucks-workers-scheduling-hours.html [accessed 17 February 2019].

23 Jannette's story is taken from Kantor, 'Working anything but 9 to 5'.

24 According to the Joseph Rowntree Foundation's 'UK poverty 2018' report (pp. 4–5), in Britain in-work poverty is at its highest for 20 years. Four million workers are in poverty, over half a million more than in 2004–5. In terms of sectors, poverty is most marked in accommodation and food services (25 per cent); https://www.jrf.org.uk/report/uk-poverty-2018 [accessed 16 February 2018].

25 Quoted in Dambisa Moyo, *The Edge of Chaos: Why Democracy is Failing to Deliver Economic Growth – and How to Fix It* (London: Little, Brown, 2018), p. xiv.

26 US manufacturing output has increased considerably since 1973 – nearly doubling in forty years – while manufacturing employment has fallen sharply – explained in large part by the entrance of China into the World Trade Organization, allowing companies to engage in global labour arbitrage and shift production to China where possible, and extracting lower wages by threatening to move jobs abroad.

27 The UK's Resolution Foundation find that labour market concentration is higher in low-paid sectors such as retail (Torsten Bell and Dan Tomlinson, 'Is everybody concentrating?', *The Resolution Foundation*, July 2018, p. 19). See also the recent issue of *The Economist* dedicated to exposing the impact of market concentration on wages (*The Economist*, 'A matter of concentration', 25 October 2018). See, in particular, the article 'Economists think anti-trust policy should pay more attention to workers'; https://www.economist.com/finance-and-economics/2018/10/25/economists-think-antitrust-policy-should-pay-more-attention-to-workersleader [accessed 25 February 2019]. In the US, meanwhile, according to the Department of Justice and Federal Trade Commission's guidelines on horizontal mergers, the average US labour market's high concentration is associated with a 17 per cent decline in posted wages. Recent research corroborates this finding.

A painstaking examination of micro-panel data of the US Economic Census (conducted every five years and examining the annual payroll of hundreds of thousands of businesses) focused on the six large sectors (manufacturing, retail trade, wholesale trade, services, finances and utilities and transportation) that make up 80 per cent of the US economy and concluded that there was a negative industry-level relationship between changes in labour share and changes in market concentration.

28   The formulation is Alan B. Krueger's and Eric A. Posner's, from their paper 'A proposal for protecting low-income workers from monopsony and collusion', *The Hamilton Project*, 27 February 2018, p. 4.

29   'Why aren't paychecks growing? a burger-joint clause offers a clue', *New York Times*, 27 September 2017; https://www.nytimes.com/2017/09/27/business/pay-growth-fast-food-hiring.html?_r=0 [accessed 21 November 2017].

30   Alan B. Krueger, Princeton economist and former president of the White House's Council of Economic Advisers, estimates that no-hire rules affect one quarter of fast-food outlets across America (quoted in 'Why aren't paychecks growing?').

31   This anecdote is taken from 'How non-compete clauses keep workers locked in', *New York Times*, 13 May 2017; https://www.nytimes.com/2017/05/13/business/noncompete-clauses.html [accessed 25 February 2019].

32   Alan B. Krueger, 'The rigged labor market', *Milten Institute Review*, 28 April 2018; http://www.milkenreview.org/articles/the-rigged-labor-market [accessed 25 February 2019].

33   I am indebted to Jonathan Tepper for alerting me to the phenomenon of monopsony and to the evidence he supplies regarding the US situation in Chapter Four of his *The Myth of Capitalism: Monopolies and the Death of Capitalism* (Hoboken, NJ: Wiley, 2019), to which I contributed research.

34   See Chapter 4 of Paul Collier's *The Future of Capitalism: Facing the New Anxieties* for an important account of

the post-war transformation of the firm, to which I am indebted.

35 Adam Smith, *An Inquiry into the Nature and Causes of the Wealth of Nations* (1776), IV.ii (Oxford: Oxford University Press, 1993), p. 292. There is much debate about the interpretation of this passage in the context of Smith's overall thought. Many argue that his account of self-interest is offset by the exhortation in other places of his work to promote the common good. For a defence of Smith against his laissez-faire appropriation see Jesse Norman's *Adam Smith: What He Thought and Why It Matters* (London: Allen Lane, 2018).

36 I think this quip is Maurice Glasman's, though to my knowledge there is no publication to cite.

37 See David Weil, *The Fissured Workplace: Why Work Became So Bad for So Many and What Can Be Done To Improve It* (Cambridge, MA: Harvard University Press, 2014).

38 According to figures compiled by the Office for National Statistics from its Labour Force Survey (covering the period October to December 2017 and published in February 2018) and results from the survey of businesses relating to November 2017.

39 The anecdote, which I paraphrase, is taken from Stephen Armstrong, *The New Poverty* (London: Verso, 2017), pp. 16–17.

40 Karl Polanyi, *The Great Transformation: The Political and Economic Origins of Our Time* ([1944] Boston, MA: Beacon Press, 2001), p. 164.

3: Sufficiency: Why the Left and Sexual Liberation Make Bad Bedfellows

1 The event was first recounted by Katie Way on babe. net, from which all quotations are taken; https://babe. net/2018/01/13/aziz-ansari-28355 [accessed 14 November 2018].

2 See Frank Trentmann's magisterial *Empire of Things: How We Became a World of Consumers, from the 15th Century to the 21st* (London: Penguin Random House, 2017).

3 William Cavanaugh, *Being Consumed* (Grand Rapids, MI: Eerdmans, 2008), p. 35.

4 Mark Greif makes this point brilliantly in his essay 'The concept of experience (the meaning of life, pt. I)', in *Against Everything* (London: Verso, 2006), p. 82.

5 Taken from Stuart Ewen, '... Images without bottom ...', in *The Consumer Society Reader*, ed. Juliet B. Schor and Douglas B. Holt (New York: W. W. Norton, 2000), p. 49.

6 Nancy Jo Sales, 'Tinder and the dawn of the "dating apocalypse"', *Vanity Fair*, 6 August 2015; https://www.vanityfair.com/culture/2015/08/tinder-hook-up-culture-end-of-dating [accessed 10 November 2018].

7 Lisa Wade, *American Hookup: The New Culture of Sex on Campus* (New York: Norton, 2017), p. 15.

8 Wilhem Reich, *The Sexual Revolution: Toward a Self-Governing Character Structure*, rev. edn, trans. T. P. Wolfe (New York: Farrar, Straus and Giroux, 1969), p. 4.

9 The story is recounted by Dominic Sandbrook in *White Heat: A History of Britain in the Swinging Sixties* (London: Abacus, 2006), p. 477.

10 Quoted in Christopher Turner, *Adventures in the Orgasmatron: The Invention of Sex* (London: Fourth Estate, 2011), p. 429.

11 Ellen Willis, 'Lust horizons: is the women's movement pro-sex?', in *No More Nice Girls: Countercultural Essays* (Minneapolis, MN: University of Minnesota Press, 1992), p. 5.

12 Greif, 'The concept of experience', p. 88.

13 Ibid., p. 89.

14 Søren Kierkegaard, *Either/Or: A Fragment of Life* (1842), trans. Alastair Hannay ([1992] London: Penguin, 2002), p. 467.

15 I owe the reference to Kierkegaard to my friend Talbot Brewer, who himself expounds the point beautifully in

his own book *The Retrieval of Ethics*: 'The rituals and repetitions of friends and lovers are never mere repetitions, because the memory of each prior enactment provides the next enactment with a subjective patina that increases its depth and resonance. Each re-enactment is like fresh writing on a half-erased chalkboard: it takes shape among and becomes entangled with its own faded forerunners, some still legible and others nearly gone from view. There is here a possibility of limitless accretion of layers of perceived meaning, hence a limitless repetition in the outward form of shared activity without a single repetition in the inner texture of the same activities' (*The Retrieval of Ethics*, Oxford: Oxford University Press, 2009, pp. 263–4).

16   Brewer, *Retrieval of Ethics*, p. 239.

17   See Juliet B. Schor, 'The commodification of childhood: tales from the advertising front lines', *The Hedgehog Review*, V:2, 2003.

18   See Mark Greif's seminal essay, 'Afternoon of the sex children', in *Against Everything*, pp. 16–36.

19   Brook, 'Traffic light tool'; https://www.brook.org.uk/our-work/the-sexual-behaviours-traffic-light-tool [accessed 13 November 2018].

20   Greif makes this point well, distinguishing between the welcome and fateful legacies of the sexual revolution – 'liberation' and 'liberalization' respectively. 'A test of liberation, as distinct from liberalization, must be whether you have also been freed to be free from sex, too – to ignore it, or to be asexual, without consequent social opprobrium or imputation of deficiency. If truly liberated you should engage in sex or not as you please, and have it be a matter of indifference to you; you should recognize your own sex, or not, whenever and however you please. We ought to see social categories of asexuals who are free to have no sex just as others are free to have endless spectacular sex, and not feel for them either suspicion or pity. *One of the cruel betrayals of sexual liberation,*

*in liberalization, was the illusion that a person can be
free only if he holds sex as all-important and exposes it
endlessly to others – providing it, proving it, enjoying it*
... This was a new kind of unfreedom' ('Afternoon of the
sex children', pp. 26–7; italics mine). What Greif misses,
in my view, is how the reason for abstinence might not
just be a lifestyle choice but a refuge from objectification
and, thus, exploitation.

21 Alexandra Schwartz, '#MeToo, #ItWasMe, and the post-
Weinstein megaphone of social media', *The New Yorker*,
19 October 2017; https://www.newyorker.com/culture/
cultural-comment/metoo-itwasme-and-the-post-weinstein-
megaphone-of-social-media [accessed 14 November 2018].
22 Ibid.

4: The Sanctity of Life: What's Pro-Life
about an AR-15?

1 https://www.facebook.com/search/posts/?q=abortion
&ref=top_filter&filters_rp_author=1045030041 [accessed
22 May 2017].
2 Daniel K. Williams, *Defenders of the Unborn: The Pro-
Life Movement before Roe v. Wade* (New York: Oxford
University Press, 2016), p. 37.
3 Ibid., p. 242.
4 James C. Mohr, *Abortion in America: The Origins and
Evolution of National Policy, 1800–1900* (New York:
Oxford University Press, 1978), pp. 147–8.
5 Quoted in Kristen Luker, *Abortion and the Politics of
Motherhood* (Berkeley and Los Angeles, CA: University of
California Press, 1984), p. 33.
6 Luker, *Abortion and the Politics of Motherhood*, p. 32.
7 Quoted in Elizabeth Dwoskin, 'Coerced abortions: a new
study shows they're common', *The Daily Beast*, 10 August
2010; https://www.thedailybeast.com/coerced-abortions-a-
new-study-shows-theyre-common [accessed 24 February
2019].

8   Meaghan Winter, 'My abortion', *New York Magazine*, 10 November 2013; http://nymag.com/news/features/abortion-stories-2013-11/index2.html [accessed 25 February 2019].

9   This is according to J. Shoshanna and Alesha E. Doan, *Abortion Regret: The New Attack on Reproductive Freedom* (Santa Barbara, CA: Praeger, 2019), p. 60.

10 Kelefa Sanneh, 'The intensity gap: can a pro-life platform win elections?', *The New Yorker*, 27 October 2014; https://www.newyorker.com/magazine/2014/10/27/intensity-gap [accessed 6 May 2019].

11 I paraphrase Peter Singer here, in his *Practical Ethics* (1980), 3rd edn (Cambridge: Cambridge University Press, 2011), p. 73.

12 'Rookie marksman wins M16 EIC match'; www.friendsofnra.org/State.aspx?sid=50&cid=931 [accessed 10 November 2015].

13 Vox, 'It's time to talk about gun control as a way to stop terrorism', 13 June 2016; https://www.vox.com/2016/6/13/11912104/terrorism-gun-control [accessed 16 May 2019].

14 http://usconservatives.about.com/od/capitalpunishment/a/Putting-Gun-Death-Statistics-In-Perspective.htm [accessed 15 November 2015].

15 https://www.cbsnews.com/news/3-children-dead-1-critically-wounded-in-separate-weekend-gun-accidents-nationwide/ [accessed 19 February 2019].

16 https://consumer.healthday.com/senior-citizen-information-31/misc-death-and-dying-news-172/more-u-s-kids-dying-from-guns-car-accidents-740809.html [accessed 6 May 2019].

17 https://injury.research.chop.edu/violence-prevention-initiative/types-violence-involving-youth/gun-violence/gun-violence-facts-and#.XGp5KdHgo0p [accessed 6 May 2019].

18 https://consumer.healthday.com/senior-citizen-information-31/misc-death-and-dying-news-172/more-u-s-kids-dying-from-guns-car-accidents-740809.html [accessed 6 May 2019].

19   'CBS Baltimore, 'Family holds vigil for three-year-old girl killed during drive-by shooting', 6 August 2014; https://baltimore.cbslocal.com/2014/08/06/funeral-set-for-toddler-shot-and-killed-during-city-drive-by-shooting/ [accessed 16 May 2019].

20   Quoted in 'NRA planning "the fight of the century" against Obama', *Washington Post*, 16 January 2013; www.washingtonpost.com/news/post-politics/wp/2013/01/16/nra-planning-the-fight-of-the-century-against-obama/ [accessed 10 November 2015].

21   I am indebted to conversation with Tal Brewer for this treatment of citizenship.

22   Quoted in https://www.washingtonpost.com/politics/put-armed-police-officers-in-every-school-nra-head-says/2012/12/21/9ac7d4ae-4b8b-11e2-9a42-d1ce6d0ed278_story.html [accessed 6 May 2019].

23   https://eu.usatoday.com/story/news/nation/2018/02/22/trump-plan-odds-teacher-armmewith-movement/362294002/ [accessed 6 May 2019].

24   See Malcolm Gladwell, *Blink: The Power of Thinking without Thinking* (London: Penguin, 2005), Chapter 6.

25   https://www.ammoland.com/2015/11/oregon-gun-control-group-reveals-prohibitionist-manifesto/#axzz5nASCSFxn [accessed 6 May 2019].

26   Quoted in James Surowiecki, 'Taking on the N.R.A.', *The New Yorker*, 19 October 2015; www.newyorker.com/magazine/2015/10/19/taking-on-the-n-r-a# [accessed 2 December 2015].

5: REVERENCE FOR NATURE: WHY GREENS SHOULDN'T BECOME CYBORGS

1   This definition is from Max More in 1990 and is quoted in 'The philosophy of transhumanism', in *The Transhumanist Reader*, ed. Max More and Natasha Vita-More (Chichester: Wiley-Blackwell, 2013), p. 3.

2 Raffi Khatchadourian, 'The philosopher of Doomsday: will
   artificial intelligence bring us Utopia or destruction?', *The
   New Yorker*, 23 November 2015.

3 To demonstrate the growing legitimacy of transhumanism,
   Khatchadourian (ibid.) makes a contrast between a
   conference for AI researchers held in Asilomar, California,
   in 2007 which 'concluded on a note of scepticism about
   the validity of the whole [AI] agenda', and a closed-door
   one in Puerto Rico in 2015, which brought together
   transhumanists with AI practitioners and legal scholars. Of
   this latter gathering he writes: '"These are not people who
   are usually in the same room," Tegmark told me ... "But
   by the time Nick's session started, people were ready to
   listen to each other." Questions that had seemed fanciful to
   researchers only seven years earlier were beginning to look
   as though they might be worth reconsidering.'

4 Quoted in Adam Rome, *The Genius of Earth Day: How
   a 1970 Teach-In Unexpectedly Made the First Green
   Revolution* (New York: Hill and Wang, 2013), p. 58.

5 https://www.nytimes.com/1990/04/16/us/veteran-of-earth-
   day-1970-looks-to-a-new-world.html [accessed 23 January
   2019].

6 Percy Mark, 'The philosophy of reverence for life and the
   Earth Charter', an essay for the Earth Charter Initiative,
   2018; http://earthcharter.org/virtual-library2/philosophy-
   reverence-life-earth-charter/ [accessed 08 May 2019].

7 William Wordsworth, *'Lines Composed a Few Miles above
   Tintern Abbey, on Revisiting the Banks of the Wye during a
   Tour'*, 13 July 1798.

8 I paraphrase Paul W. Taylor here, from his *Respect for Nature:
   A Theory of Environmental Ethics* ([1986] Princeton, NJ:
   Princeton University Press, 2011), p. 116.

9 Quoted in Theodor W. Adorno and Max Horkheimer,
   Dialectic of Enlightenment ([1944] London: Verso, 1997),
   pp. 3–4.

10 Ibid.

11 Herbert Marcuse, *One-Dimensional Man: Studies in the Ideology of Advanced Industrial Society*, 2nd edn (London and New York: Routledge, 2002), p. 157.

12 I paraphrase Wendell Berry here, in his essay 'Total economy' (1980), in *The World-Ending Fire: The Essential Wendell Berry*, ed. Paul Kingsnorth (London: Allen Lane, 2017), p. 66.

13 David Wallace-Wells, *The Uninhabitable Earth: A History of the Future* (London: Allen Lane, 2019), pp. 154–5.

14 Max More, 'Letter to Mother Nature', in *The Transhumanism Reader: Classical and Contemporary Essays on the Science, Technology, and Philosophy of the Human Future*, ed. Max More and Natasha Vita-More (Oxford: Wiley-Blackwell, 2013), pp. 449–50.

15 'Introduction', *The Transhumanism Reader*, p. 4.

16 Quoted in Hubert L. Dreyfus, *On the Internet* (2001), 2nd edn (Abingdon: Routledge, 2009), p. 4.

17 Matthew B. Crawford, *The World beyond Your Head: Becoming an Individual in an Age of Distraction* (New York: Farrar, Straus and Giroux, 2015), p. 23.

18 Ibid.

19 Ibid., pp. 86–7.

20 According to proponents of the Singularity thesis, the belief in a future moment when computing power reaches an 'intelligence explosion', the only way humans will be able to survive the technological forces they have unleashed is by themselves merging with technology. The body will be substituted with a whole-brain 'emulation' as – and the technical details are complicated – neural networks of a person's brain are scanned, reconstructed, converted into a computational model and then emulated on an independent substrate.

21 Quoted in 'DNA pioneer urges gene free-for-all,' *The Guardian*, 9 April 2003; https://www.theguardian.com/science/2003/apr/09/genetics.research [accessed 22 February 2019].

22 Yuval Noah Harari, *Homo Deus: A Brief History of Tomorrow* (London: Vintage, 2016), p. 63.
23 See Daniel Groll and Micah Lott, 'Is there a role for "human nature" in debates about human enhancement?', *Philosophy* 90:4 (2015).
24 The anecdote is from 'The philosopher of Doomsday'.
25 Jennifer Doudna and Samuel Sternberg, *A Crack in Creation: The New Power to Control Evolution* (London: Bodley Head, 2017), p. 239.
26 The quotation is from Fraser Nelson's excellent article 'The Return of Eugenics', *The Spectator*, 2 April 2016.

6: Personal Responsibility: Why the Right Should Release Ex-Offenders

1 The anecdote is taken from the ACLU; https://www.aclu.org/other/words-prison-collateral-consequences-incarceration [accessed 28 March 2019].
2 Yascha Mounk, *The Age of Responsibility: Luck, Choice and the Welfare State* (Cambridge, MA: Harvard University Press, 2017), p. 1.
3 David Cameron, 'Return to responsibility', *The Guardian*, 27 February 2010; https://www.theguardian.com/commentisfree/2010/feb/27/david-cameron-personal-responsibility [accessed 28 March 2019].
4 Quoted in Mounck, *The Age of Responsibility*, p. 2.
5 Simone Weil, *The Need for Roots* ([1949] New York: Routledge, 2002), p. 15.
6 I am indebted to Philip Lorish for this discussion of agency.
7 Quoted in Mounk, *The Age of Responsibility*, p. 148.
8 Oliver O'Donovan, *Self, World and Time* (Grand Rapids, MI: Eerdmans, 2013), p. 2.
9 Michael J. Formica, 'Addiction, self-responsibility and the importance of choice', *Psychology Today*, 3 June 2010; https://www.psychologytoday.com/gb/blog/enlightened-living/201006/addiction-self-responsibility-and-the-importance-choice [accessed 25 May 2019].

10   'Shelley's success story'; https://www.theprocessrecovery
     center.com/drug-alcohol-addiction-success-stories/shelleys-
     success-story/ [accessed 11 May 2019].

11   Georgia Apartment Association, 'Application for occupancy';
     https://images.frmonline.com/imgs/fr/propertyFiles/
     667/000/1/05_12360883520129381.pdf [accessed 28
     March 2019], p. 2.

12   I paraphrase Jeremy Travis here, from his article 'Invisible
     punishment: an instrument of social exclusion', in *Invisible
     Punishment: The Collateral Consequences of Mass
     Imprisonment*, ed. Marc Mauer and Meda Chesney-Lind
     (New York: The New Press, 2002), p. 18.

13   Gabriel J. Chin, 'The new civil death: rethinking punishment
     in the era of mass incarceration', *University of Pennsylvania
     Law Review*, 160:6 (Symposium: Sentencing Law: Rhetoric
     and Reality), May 2012, pp. 1790–91.

14   Travis, 'Invisible punishment', p. 21.

15   Bureau of Justice Statistics, 'Correctional populations in the
     U.S., 2016', April 2018; https://www.bjs.gov/content/pub/
     pdf/cpus16.pdf [accessed 11 May 2019].

16   Quoted in ACLU, 'Mass incarceration'; https://www.aclu.
     org/issues/smart-justice/mass-incarceration [accessed 11 May
     2019].

17   'Employees with criminal records deserve a second chance',
     New York Law Journal, 24 August 2018; https://www.
     law.com/newyorklawjournal/2018/08/24/employees-
     with-criminal-records-deserve-a-second-chance/?slretu
     rn=20190411085138 [accessed 11 May 2019].

18   Michelle Alexander, *The New Jim Crow: Mass Incarceration
     in the Age of Colorblindness*, rev. edn (New York: The New
     Press, 2012), p. 141.

19   The anecdote is taken from Jacob Sullum's article 'The
     lingering stench of marijuana prohibition', *Reason*, March
     2019; http://reason.com/archives/2019/03/01/the-lingering-
     stench-of-mariju [accessed 07 March 2019].

20   Anecdote sourced in Center for American Progress, 'One
     strike and you're out: how we can eliminate barriers to

economic security and mobility for people with criminal records', December 2014; https://cdn.americanprogress.org/wp-content/uploads/2014/12/VallasCriminalRecords Report.pdf [accessed 7 March 2019].

21 *United States District Court Eastern District of New York, United States of America, v. Chevelle Nesbet*, Opinion 15-CR-18 FB, p. 11; https://www.nytimes.com/interactive/2016/05/25/nyregion/document-Federal-Judge-on-Impact-of-Felony-Convictions.html?module=inline [accessed 28 March 2019].

22 Zachary Hoskins and Nora Wikoff, 'Hard times after hard time', in *The Wire and Philosophy: This America, Man*, ed. David Bzdak, Joanna Crosby and Seth Vannatta (Chicago, IL: Open Court, 2013), p. 180.

23 I am indebted for this whole reflection on agency to Alasdair MacIntyre's discussion of the import of his seminal book *Dependent Rational Animals* in *Conversations on Ethics*, ed. Alex Voorhoeve (Oxford: Oxford University Press, 2009), p. 120.

24 Quoted in The Centre for Social Justice, *Meaningful Mentoring*, April 2014, p. 7.

25 The anecdote is taken from The National Reentry Resource Centre, 'Second chance act spotlight: Darius Dennis, Norfolk, Virginia', 13 September 2017; https://csgjusticecenter.org/nrrc/posts/second-chance-act-spotlight-darius-dennis-norfolk-virginia/ [accessed 28 March 2019].

26 Ben's story is taken by Noel Titheradge's article, 'Lost in the system', for BBC News; https://www.bbc.co.uk/news/resources/idt-sh/Lost_in_a_system [accessed 15 February 2019].

27 Hoskins and Wikoff, 'Hard times after hard time', p. 181.

CONCLUSION: MORAL IMAGINATION

1 I take this example from the essay to which this chapter is indebted, David Bromwich, 'Moral imagination', in *Moral Imagination: Essays* (Princeton, NJ: Princeton University Press, 2014), pp. 13–17.

2   Bromwich, 'Moral imagination', pp. 26, 13.

3   Quoted in 'In the gun debate, it's urban vs. rural', *USA Today*, 27 February 2013; https://eu.usatoday.com/story/news/nation/2013/02/27/guns-ingrained-in-rural-existence/1949479/ [accessed 23 February 2019].

4   John Arras, 'Physician-assisted suicide: a tragic view', in *Ethical Issues in Modern Medicine: Contemporary Readings in Bioethics*, 8th edn, ed. Bonnie Steinbock, Alex John London and John D. Arras (New York: McGraw-Hill, 2013), p. 459.

5   Kwame Anthony Appiah, *Cosmopolitanism: Ethics in a World of Strangers* (London: Penguin, 2006), p. xiii. I am indebted here to Appiah's account of cosmopolitanism, from which I borrow quotations.

6   Galatians 3:28.

7   Quoted in Appiah, *Cosmopolitanism*, p. xiii.

8   Yuval Noah Harari, *21 Lessons for the 21st Century* (London: Penguin, 2018), p. 224.

9   Quoted in Mary Midgley, 'Evolutionary dramas', in *The Essential Mary Midgley*, ed. David Midgley (Oxford: Routledge, 2005), pp. 241–2.

10 David Sloane Wilson, *Does Altruism Exist? Culture, Genes, and the Welfare of Others* (New Haven, CT, and London: Yale University Press, 2015), p. 4 (italics mine).

11 David Bentley Hart, *The Experience of God: Being, Consciousness, Bliss* (New Haven, CT: Yale University Press, 2013), p. 265.

12 Jonathan Haidt, *The Righteous Mind: Why Good People are Divided by Politics and Religion* (New York: Vintage, p. 2012), p. 284.

PERMISSIONS

INDEX

NOTE ON THE AUTHOR

James Mumford lives in London and is a fellow at the University of Virginia's Institute for Advanced Studies in Culture. He received his PhD from Oxford University and was a Henry fellow at Yale where his graduate studies were in political philosophy and religion. He has written for the *Guardian, New Statesman, Atlantic, Spectator, Daily Telegraph* and *The Times Literary Supplement*.

@JamesACMumford / jamesmumford.co.uk

NOTE ON THE TYPE

The text of this book is set in Linotype Sabon, a typeface named after the type founder, Jacques Sabon. It was designed by Jan Tschichold and jointly developed by Linotype, Monotype and Stempel in response to a need for a typeface to be available in identical form for mechanical hot metal composition and hand composition using foundry type.

Tschichold based his design for Sabon roman on a font engraved by Garamond, and Sabon italic on a font by Granjon. It was first used in 1966 and has proved an enduring modern classic.